Samuel French Acting Edition

Lie, Cheat, and Genuflect

by Billy Van Zandt
and Jane Milmore

SAMUELFRENCH.COM   SAMUELFRENCH.CO.UK

Copyright © 2019 by Billy Van Zandt and Jane Milmore
All Rights Reserved

LIE, CHEAT, AND GENUFLECT is fully protected under the copyright laws of the United States of America, the British Commonwealth, including Canada, and all member countries of the Berne Convention for the Protection of Literary and Artistic Works, the Universal Copyright Convention, and/or the World Trade Organization conforming to the Agreement on Trade Related Aspects of Intellectual Property Rights. All rights, including professional and amateur stage productions, recitation, lecturing, public reading, motion picture, radio broadcasting, television and the rights of translation into foreign languages are strictly reserved.

ISBN 978-0-573-61875-8

www.SamuelFrench.com
www.SamuelFrench.co.uk

FOR PRODUCTION ENQUIRIES

UNITED STATES AND CANADA
Info@SamuelFrench.com
1-866-598-8449

UNITED KINGDOM AND EUROPE
Plays@SamuelFrench.co.uk
020-7255-4302

Each title is subject to availability from Samuel French, depending upon country of performance. Please be aware that *LIE, CHEAT, AND GENUFLECT* may not be licensed by Samuel French in your territory. Professional and amateur producers should contact the nearest Samuel French office or licensing partner to verify availability.

CAUTION: Professional and amateur producers are hereby warned that *LIE, CHEAT, AND GENUFLECT* is subject to a licensing fee. Publication of this play(s) does not imply availability for performance. Both amateurs and professionals considering a production are strongly advised to apply to Samuel French before starting rehearsals, advertising, or booking a theater. A licensing fee must be paid whether the title(s) is presented for charity or gain and whether or not admission is charged. Professional/Stock licensing fees are quoted upon application to Samuel French.

No one shall make any changes in this title(s) for the purpose of production. No part of this book may be reproduced, stored in a retrieval system, or transmitted in any form, by any means, now known or yet to be invented, including mechanical, electronic, photocopying, recording, videotaping, or otherwise, without the prior written permission of the publisher. No one shall upload this title(s), or part of this title(s), to any social media websites.

For all enquiries regarding motion picture, television, and other media rights, please contact Samuel French.

MUSIC USE NOTE

Licensees are solely responsible for obtaining formal written permission from copyright owners to use copyrighted music in the performance of this play and are strongly cautioned to do so. If no such permission is obtained by the licensee, then the licensee must use only original music that the licensee owns and controls. Licensees are solely responsible and liable for all music clearances and shall indemnify the copyright owners of the play(s) and their licensing agent, Samuel French, against any costs, expenses, losses and liabilities arising from the use of music by licensees. Please contact the appropriate music licensing authority in your territory for the rights to any incidental music.

IMPORTANT BILLING AND CREDIT REQUIREMENTS

If you have obtained performance rights to this title, please refer to your licensing agreement for important billing and credit requirements.

LIE, CHEAT, AND GENUFLECT opened August 21, 1981, at the Dam Site Dinner-Theatre, Tinton Falls, New Jersey, under the direction of William Van Zandt. The play was produced by Kathy Reed. Original set design was by Russell Schiavone. Lighting and sound were by Ed McGuire. The cast, in order of appearance, was as follows:

BILLY BUCKLE	Billy Van Zandt
TOM BUCKLE	Bill Introcaso
ROBERT FRYBURGER	Brian Fuorry
VIRGINIA	Kay Stansbury
GIRL	Pam D'Amato
JANE	Jane Milmore
PIZZA FACE PETRILLO	Russ Gibson
MISS MACKINTOSH	Lucille A. Lo Sapio*

*Subsequent performances played by Kathy Reed

CHARACTERS

BILLY BUCKLE
TOM BUCKLE
ROBERT FRYBURGER
VIRGINIA
GIRL
JANE
PIZZA FACE PETRILLO
MISS MACKINTOSH

SETTING

Library at Buckle Manor in Deal, New Jersey.

TIME

The present.

ACT I

(At Rise: It is night. About eleven. We see two figures descend the stairwell, dressed in black. Each holds a flashlight. The room is full of dust and cobwebs. Drop cloths cover the furniture, but we can make out a sofa and a table and chair, all down stage. The two figures separate and scan the room with their lights. They follow around and flash their lights into each other's eyes. They shriek and jump.)

TOM. What's the matter with you?

BILLY. I'm scared. You scared me.

TOM. Well, be scared so nobody can hear you!

BILLY. I hardly remember this place. I must have been five years old the last time I was in here.

TOM. I was seven, but I remember everything. I remember where grandfather's lab is, where the workshop is, where the secret passages are. I've got every inch of this place up here.

(He indicates his head.)

BILLY. How did you remember all that?

TOM. I climbed the trellis yesterday and went through the house. I found this map in one of the rooms upstairs.

(He pulls a blueprint out of his hat. They study it with their lights.)

BILLY. I don't like this Tom, we're trespassing.

TOM. It's only called trespassing when somebody lives there. Now that grandfather's...

BILLY. Dead?

TOM. Yes. Now that nobody lives here, there's nothing illegal about it. We're not trespassing, we're just looking.

BILLY. If there's nothing illegal about it, why are we dressed in black in the dark with flashlights?

TOM. Because you and I know we're just looking. The police may not see it that way.

BILLY. Oh. Now will you tell me why we illegally entered grandfather's house to "just look"?

TOM. Tomorrow is the reading of grandfather's will, right?

BILLY. Right.

TOM. There are only three living relatives, right?

BILLY. Right.

TOM. You, me, and that girl Lisa.

BILLY. Right.

TOM. What do you think the odds are that we are going to be left a red cent?

BILLY. Grandfather hated our family. We won't be left a nickel.

TOM. Right. That's what we're doing in here. We're going to find and take home what is rightfully ours.

BILLY. That's stealing.

TOM. It's not stealing, exactly.

BILLY. What is it, exactly?

TOM. Borrowing. We're merely going to borrow what should rightfully be ours in the first place. Afterwards we can give it all back.

BILLY. After what? What are we borrowing?

TOM. We're going to find the safe and take a large portion of money.

BILLY. I can't do that. I've never done anything illegal in my life. I don't even need money. I have a large savings account. I'll lend some to you. Please, let's leave.

TOM. You can't lend some to me.

BILLY. Sure I can. I trust you.

TOM. I meant you can't lend some to me because you haven't got any.

BILLY. I most certainly do. I've had you put away money for me every week for the past five years. My goodness, I must have saved up over...why are you shaking your head?

TOM. How can you tell I'm shaking my head in the dark?

BILLY. Where's my money?

TOM. I've been meaning to tell you... I kind of bet some of your savings on the horses.

BILLY. You've been betting my money?

TOM. *(Covering his mouth.)* Sshh!

BILLY. This is a fine time to tell me. How much is some of?

TOM. ...Some of is more like "all of." You're broker than I am.

BILLY. How can that be?

TOM. You owe Pizza Face Petrillo $4,000.

BILLY. You gambled my entire life savings away at the track?

TOM. You're not listening. It wasn't at the track. I kind of owe a loan shark a lot of money. You too.

BILLY. Me too? I don't even know Pizza Face Whatever-His-Name-Is.

TOM. All we needed was one winner. Then we could have retired from the oil industry.

BILLY. "Oil industry"? You make it sound like we own Exxon.

TOM. It's better than telling people we pump gas. I was just trying to take care of you.

BILLY. Nevermind. How much do we owe this guy?

TOM. Well, you owe him $4,000. And I owe him $120.

BILLY. I'm going to kill you.

TOM. It's not my fault. They were sure-bets. I had hot tips.

BILLY. So we're here to steal grandfather's money to pay off some mobster?

TOM. "Borrow." Tomorrow we make one more bet, and win enough to pay back the inheritance to Lisa...and nobody is the wiser.

BILLY. Especially you! What if we lose this bet, tomorrow? Then we owe Lisa and the Mob.

TOM. What choice do we have? If we don't pay up by tomorrow, we're going to go for a swim in the East River. We'll go for a one-way ride. We'll be fitted with cement boots...

BILLY. I get the picture.

TOM. I'm going to look upstairs. You check around down here.

BILLY. No. I don't want to. I'm afraid.

TOM. There's nothing to fear but fear itself.

>   *(We hear a blood-curdling scream off – upstage right.* **BILLY** *leaps into* **TOM***'s arms.)*

BILLY. What was that?

TOM. Fear Itself. Someone's hiding. Come.

BILLY. What?

TOM. I mean someone's coming. Hide.
Quick. Under the drop cloths.

>   *(***TOM*** hides under the drop cloth stage left, sitting on the chair.* **BILLY** *sits on the sofa, under that drop cloth. Through the upstage right archway, an anxious young man in his thirties enters – briefcase in hand. He is followed by a homely old woman in a maid uniform. Her make-up is thick and makes her look embalmed.* **ROBERT FRYBURGER***, attorney, and* **VIRGINIA***, sex-starved alcoholic maid.)*

FRYBURGER. *(Snapping on the lights.)* The old place looks the same as ever, Virginia.

VIRGINIA. I haven't touched a thing since Mr. Buckle passed on.

FRYBURGER. Yes, I noticed. I'm sorry I frightened you, Virginia. I keep forgetting that you still live here. I should have knocked.

VIRGINIA. That's quite all right. I don't mind staying here. I have my spirits to keep me company.

FRYBURGER. Spirits?

VIRGINIA. Voices from beyond the grave. Mr. Buckle talks to me. The man was a genius, Mr. Fryburger, a genius! The common belt buckle. Today we take it for granted but imagine the mind that must have been behind its creation. Theodore Buckle's great-great-grandfather.

FRYBURGER. How does someone think up such a creation?

VIRGINIA. They say his pants kept falling down.

> (**VIRGINIA** *eyes* **FRYBURGER** *and begins to flirt with him.*)

FRYBURGER. And to wind up dead as a result of further exploration in the field of buckles. It's a shame.

VIRGINIA. Yessir. He died in the line of duty.

FRYBURGER. Now, Virginia, the descendants will be arriving tomorrow at about 3:00. Please have the house in order.

VIRGINIA. Mr. Buckle had no living relatives. I doubt anyone will be coming. I'm the only heir. If you'll excuse me, I've got to go clean out the wine cellar.

FRYBURGER. Don't play innocent with me. There are three relatives. His adopted granddaughter Lisa from his third marriage. And those other two from his first marriage.

VIRGINIA. We weren't permitted to talk about that side of the family in this house.

FRYBURGER. Thomas T. Buckle and William F. Buckle.

VIRGINIA. The sons of that idiot. I won't discuss them. They were forbidden to set foot in this house while Mr. Buckle was alive. I haven't seen them in seventeen years.

FRYBURGER. Virginia, tell me...what did John Buckle do to become the black sheep of the family? What could he have possibly done to become so hated by his father?

VIRGINIA. He opened a suspender store! He's the one, you know. He's the one responsible for Mr. Buckle's...

FRYBURGER. Death?

VIRGINIA. Yes. That no good bum showed up after seventeen years to try and sell his father on an idea for an electronic belt buckle. When I heard the explosion it was too late.

FRYBURGER. How did he get into the house?

VIRGINIA. He climbed the trellis and surprised Mr. Buckle in his bath. I barely made it out of there alive.

FRYBURGER. What a shame. What about the adopted granddaughter Lisa?

VIRGINIA. Haven't seen her in fifteen years. When her father passed on, she was sent off to boarding schools. She was such a cute little girl. She must be a beautiful young lady today.

> (**VIRGINIA** *reaches behind a book in the bookcase and pulls out a bottle of booze, taking a gulp.*)

Drink?

FRYBURGER. Can I have a glass with it?

VIRGINIA. Sure. Sit down. I'll fix you a drink.

> (**FRYBURGER** *sits on* **TOM**, *disguised as a chair. He reacts to how uncomfortable it is.*)

FRYBURGER. Why do you stay on here, Virginia? With Mr. Buckle...

VIRGINIA. Dead.

FRYBURGER. Yes. There's nothing to keep you here.

VIRGINIA. There certainly is. I haven't finished cleaning out the wine cellar yet.

> (**VIRGINIA** *drains the bottle dry.*)

FRYBURGER. How about that drink, Virginia? You really are cleaning out the wine cellar, aren't you?

VIRGINIA. *(Choking.)* Smooth! Ah!

(Hides bottle back in wall.)

(She poses at the bookcase, flirting at **FRYBURGER**. *She walks to the sofa, seductively.)*

Haven't seen you around here in a while, Mr. Fryburger.

(She sits on **BILLY**, *showing off her legs to an uninterested lawyer.)*

Not since Mr. Buckle...

FRYBURGER. Died!

VIRGINIA. Yes. He was a saint, that man. A saint! I devoted my life to him. It's hard to believe he's...

FRYBURGER. Dead!

VIRGINIA. Yes. I'll never forget his last words to me as I went running from the tub. "Virginia," he said, "forget the will. Take everything I own." What a saint! It's been so quiet around here since he...since he...

FRYBURGER. Died!!

VIRGINIA. Yes.

FRYBURGER. This should all be very interesting, this will business. The heirs will not leave here empty-handed. Mr. Buckle has all of his wealth divided up and the heirs will be leaving here with cash in their hands.

VIRGINIA. Mr. Buckle hated red tape. By any chance, do you know who the cash will be going to?

FRYBURGER. I'm sorry, Virginia. But a lawyer is like a doctor and a priest. I have an oath of secrecy. Besides, no one has seen the will since it's been sealed. This is my first case since passing the Bar Exam and they told me I couldn't peek.

*(***FRYBURGER*** sits at the sofa. We hear* **BILLY** *from underneath.)*

BILLY. Uh.

FRYBURGER. What was that?

VIRGINIA. I didn't hear anything.

FRYBURGER. I definitely heard an "uh."

BILLY. Uh!

FRYBURGER. There it is again!

VIRGINIA. It's Mr. Buckle! He's calling us from beyond the grave!

FRYBURGER. *(Getting nervous.)* You're imagining things.

VIRGINIA. *(Rising.)* Speak to us! Mr. Buckle, speak to us! Reach out to us and speak!

> *(She re-sits on BILLY.)*

What have you got to say to us?

BILLY. GetupforGod'ssake! Get up!

VIRGINIA. He spoke! He spoke!

FRYBURGER. Stop trying to spook me, woman! Where's that drink?

VIRGINIA. Down in the wine cellar. I could have sworn I heard a voice.

FRYBURGER. Well, I didn't hear anything.

> *(He quickly gathers his papers and briefcase.)*

I'm coming with you. Are there a lot of bright lights down there?

VIRGINIA. Why?

FRYBURGER. I, er, wouldn't want you to trip.

> *(He looks back over his shoulder at the "spirits.")*

VIRGINIA. *(Flirting back.)* Why, Mr. Fryburger!

> *(He drops her hand in repulsion. They exit into wine cellar.)*

TOM. *(Under drop.)* Billy? Psst. Billy, can you hear me?

BILLY. Yeah.

> *(**TOM** rises, dropping the drop cloth.)*

TOM. They're gone. Quick. Get up.

BILLY. *(Under drop.)* I can't. I have cramps in my legs.

> *(**TOM** throws off the drop cloth and helps him stand. His legs are like rubber.)*

TOM. Did you hear all that? Stand up!

BILLY. My leg petrified.

TOM. I have good news for you. We're not going to rob grandfather.

BILLY. Good, let's get out of here.

TOM. Will you stand up? Listen to me. We haven't got much time.

BILLY. For what?

TOM. We're going to kidnap Lisa.

BILLY. I don't think I heard you correctly. I thought I heard you say we were going to kidnap our cousin.

TOM. Well, that's what I did say. Well, not kidnap exactly.

BILLY. Then what, exactly?

TOM. We're just going to kind of borrow her.

BILLY. Again with the borrowing. We borrow our cousin. We borrow from loan sharks. What else are we going to borrow?

TOM. Novacaine from grandfather's lab.

BILLY. For what? You have a toothache?

TOM. No, I don't have a toothache. We're going to stick Lisa with a needle of novacaine so she can't walk and hole her up in the wall.

BILLY. I'm getting out of here.

TOM. Oh no, you don't. You're in this with me. And right up to your throat. Hear me out. All we have to do is knock out Lisa when she shows up here. We stick her with novacaine so she can't walk and we hide her in a secret passage somewhere behind that bookcase. Then when the will is read and the money is doled out, we leave – pay off the loan shark – and have enough left for one final bet which will earn us enough to pay back Lisa when everything's finished. It can't miss. It's a sure bet!

BILLY. Oh, that's all we're going to do? What are you, crazy? We'll go to jail for kidnapping.

TOM. Look, we are in a desperate situation here. There's no other way. Don't worry. I have everything worked out. It's foolproof.

BILLY. You have what worked out? If we stick Lisa in a wall somewhere, how is she supposed to collect her share of the inheritance? They're not going to just let you borrow her portion.

TOM. Oh, well, that's easy to fix. We have a substitute Lisa show up to collect the money.

BILLY. That might work.

TOM. Of course it will work. You heard Virginia. No one has seen the girl in over fifteen years. They'll have no idea what she looks like.

BILLY. That would work. Boy, throw a drop cloth over your head and you can really think.

TOM. Thank you. Now, when you show up claiming to be Lisa…

BILLY. Hold it. Wait a minute. Run that by me again.

TOM. Okay. We stick Lisa with a needle of novacaine.

BILLY. Not that part. The other part. The part I didn't hear correctly. When I show up claiming to be who?

TOM. Whom.

BILLY. "Whom" am I going to claim to be?

TOM. Who.

BILLY. I'll kill you if you don't answer me.

TOM. Now, Billy, listen. You're absolutely right. Lisa's got to show up to claim her money. So naturally, you're the one to fill that duty.

BILLY. I'm getting out of here. Why am I naturally the one?

TOM. You have to do it.

BILLY. I'd rather go to jail. I'm not going to get away with that. I have to show up here myself, don't I?

TOM. We'll hide a change of clothes for you upstairs and you can keep on changing.

BILLY. It won't work. I don't look remotely like a girl. How many girls do you know with hair all over their chests?

TOM. Two. Now, don't worry about a thing. I'll handle all the details. You simply make an appearance, collect your money and split.

BILLY. How about the details of Lisa's life? I haven't seen her in seventeen years. I'm out of touch with whatever she's been doing. What if they checked my background?

TOM. I'm way ahead of you. I know a way they'll be unable to retrace your steps as Lisa Buckle.

BILLY. How?

TOM. We simply tell them that you are a nun. That way...

BILLY. You're sick. You are a sick person. How do you think of things like that. Something is wrong with you. Let me get this straight. You want to take an innocent girl that we don't even know, stick her with novacaine so she can't walk in a wall, and have me dress up like a nun so we can pay off a mobster for debts I didn't even make. Is that what you want me to do?

TOM. Well, yes. More or less.

BILLY. I'm getting out of here.

> (**TOM** *grabs* **BILLY** *by the seat of his pants and he runs in place.*)

You take her place. This was your bright idea. You be the nun.

> (**BILLY** *shakes free but doesn't run out.*)

A nun? How did you ever come up with that?

TOM. I saw *The Sound of Music* on TV last night. I'm really proud of myself. This is a great plan.

BILLY. You be the nun!

TOM. Look, I thought of the plan. This is the least you can do.

BILLY. Why? Why do I have to do it?

TOM. You look more like a nun than I do.

BILLY. Oh, well, that's different. What's that supposed to mean?

TOM. How many nuns do you know with big black mustaches?

BILLY. Three.

TOM. Come on, we haven't got much time. Let's get upstairs and find the lab so we can get the novacaine.

BILLY. Give me one good reason I should do this. Give me one good reason.

TOM. If we don't pay Pizza Face Petrillo his money by tomorrow, he's going to have us killed.

BILLY. That's good enough for me. Let's go.

> (*We hear offstage laughter coming from the wine cellar.*)

TOM. Quick. The drop cloths.

> (**TOM** *heads back for his chair, but* **BILLY** *pulls him back, insisting they trade positions.*)

BILLY. This time, I'm going over there!

> (*As* **TOM** *and* **BILLY** *disguise themselves under the drop cloths,* **FRYBURGER** *and* **VIRGINIA** *enter, carrying bottles, soused. They swagger.*)

FRYBURGER. This is good stuff! Hello spirits! Virginia, why do you stay on here? There's nothing to hold you here. You were paid right up until the day Mr. Buckle…

VIRGINIA. Died.

FRYBURGER. Yes.

VIRGINIA. I haven't gotten my two weeks notice yet.

FRYBURGER. (*Leaning on the back of* **BILLY.**) How do you expect him to give you notice?

VIRGINIA. I'm staying right here until he tells me I'm fired. And if you don't like it, you can just drop…

FRYBURGER. Dead?

VIRGINIA. Yes.

FRYBURGER. Tell me, were you in the bathroom with Mr. Buckle when he went?

VIRGINIA. No, but I was there when he took his bath.

FRYBURGER. That's what I meant. Were you with him when he took his last fatal bath?

VIRGINIA. I was the last thing he saw before he…
FRYBURGER. Died.
VIRGINIA. Yes.
FRYBURGER. What a way to go.

> (**FRYBURGER** *sits on* **BILLY**.)

VIRGINIA. He had such a weak heart. He was a delicate man, really. He'd had seven heart attacks before his untimely death at the age of ninety-seven. I was there for every one of them.
FRYBURGER. Do you remember your last words to him? You know, before his idiot son burst into the room with the electronic belt buckle?
VIRGINIA. My last words to him? I remember very well. I said, "BOO!" It was a little game we used to play.

> (**FRYBURGER**'s *head drops back. He is fast asleep.*)

That old fool better have left me something. No man sleeps with me and doesn't remember me for it. Mr. Fryburger? Mr. Fryburger…
FRYBURGER. ZZZzzzz.
VIRGINIA. Mr. Fryburger, are you asleep?

> (*She looks around to make sure the coast is clear. She dives into* **FRYBURGER**'s *lap and snuggles up close. We hear* **BILLY** *wince in pain.*)

BILLY. Oh!
VIRGINIA. Forgive me, Mr. Buckle!

> (*She konks out, snoring along with* **FRYBURGER**.)

TOM. Psst. Billy. Billy? Are they asleep?
BILLY. (*High-pitched.*) Yes.

> (**TOM** *rises, removing his drop cloth.*)

TOM. Okay, I'll go get the novacaine. I've got a lot to do tonight. I've got to find a nun suit. I've got to study my map. I'll come by for you in the morning.

>*(**TOM** is halfway out the doorway, and turns back to **BILLY**.)*

Where am I going to find a nun suit at this time of night?

>*(He exits with his map and flashlight.)*

BILLY. *(After a beat.)* Tom. Tom! Oh Tom?!

>*(The bodies start to sink a little lower in the chair.)*
>
>*(Blackout.)*

Scene Two

(It is the next day, about 3:00. The drop cloths have been removed, exposing old Victorian furniture. The decanters at the bar are filled. A tray, uncovered, offers hors d'oeuvres. **VIRGINIA** *enters the room, all bubbly, followed by a hunched over* **FRYBURGER**. *His back aches from his lousy night's sleep.)*

VIRGINIA. Isn't it a beautiful day, Bob?

FRYBURGER. My name is Mr. Fryburger. And no it isn't a beautiful day. My back is killing me. Why didn't you wake me up? That was the worst night's sleep I ever had.

VIRGINIA. You looked so peaceful. I didn't want to disturb you.

FRYBURGER. That chair. It was like sleeping on a pile of bones.

(He sets his briefcase down stage left. **VIRGINIA** *eyes him behind his back.)*

I had these dreams, Virginia. Weird dreams. Strange dreams. I dreamt I was attacked by vampires all night long. Blood sucking vampires. And when I woke up this morning, look what I found when I looked in the mirror. Look. Look at my neck. What do you see?

VIRGINIA. You need a shave.

(Doorbell. **VIRGINIA** *leaves to answer the door.* **FRYBURGER** *opens his briefcase, straightens his back out and bids hello to the spirits.)*

FRYBURGER. Hello Mr. Buckle.

*(***TOM** *and* **BILLY**, *in ill-fitting suits, enter.* **BILLY** *walks as hunched over as* **FRYBURGER**. **TOM** *is cheery and cocky.* **BILLY** *carries two suitcases.)*

FRYBURGER. Gentlemen!

> (**TOM** *and* **BILLY** *look behind them.*)

How do you do. I'm Robert Fryburger. Your grandfather's attorney.

BILLY. I'm Billy Buckle. My grandfather's grandson.

TOM. *(Hunching over to meet their height.)* How do you do, Mr. Fryburger. I'm Thomas T. Buckle.

FRYBURGER. What does the T stand for?

TOM. Father used to play a lot of golf.

> *(They shake hands.)*

Shake hands with the man, Billy.

BILLY. Oh.

> (**BILLY** *goes to shake hands, but his hands are full. He hands both suitcases to* **FRYBURGER**, *then goes to shake his hand.* **FRYBURGER** *cannot return the shake, his hands being full. He drops the suitcases in disgust.*)

FRYBURGER. I've heard a lot about you two. You're exactly what I had pictured. But somehow I thought you'd be taller. I hope you had a pleasant trip up.

TOM. Lovely.

BILLY. Hey. Look, my thumb got sunburned.

> *(He shows* **TOM**, *who slaps it away.*)

TOM. It was such a beautiful day we thought we'd walk up.

FRYBURGER. We're waiting for your cousin Lisa and then we'll get started with the will business.

TOM. That sounds fine, Mr. Fryburger. Doesn't it, Billy?

BILLY. Yes, fine.

FRYBURGER. You must be anxious to see Lisa again. From what I understand, you haven't seen each other for over fifteen years.

TOM. That's right. No one has seen her.

FRYBURGER. She was difficult to track down. There wasn't any address on her. In fact, if she hadn't called our office we'd never have found her.

TOM. Greedy kid.

FRYBURGER. She didn't seem that way to me. But then I only spoke with her long enough to give her my condolences and give her this address.

TOM. She didn't mention what she's been up to for these past fifteen years, did she?

FRYBURGER. No. Very secretive girl.

TOM. Not with us. She writes us all the time. Right Billy?

BILLY. She does?

TOM. Yes, she does! Forgive Billy, Mr. Fryburger. He can't read.

FRYBURGER. What has Lisa been up to?

TOM. Our dear cousin Lisa has been called to the church. She's now a woman of the cloth. A nun. That's probably why you couldn't track her down. They give up their past lives when they enter the church. She even has a new name now. The former Lisa Buckle is now called by the name of Sister Angelica...

BILLY. Agnes...

TOM. Catherine...

BILLY. Fernando...

TOM. Bertrille.

FRYBURGER. *(Writing.)* Sister Angelica Agnes Catherine Fernando Bertrille. That's a very long name.

TOM. Well, she's been a nun a very long time.

FRYBURGER. Virginia tells me that Lisa was a beautiful child. She must be absolutely ravishing today.

(**BILLY** *reacts, smoothing his hair.*)

TOM. Well, I wouldn't count on it. From what we've heard, she's gotten real homely in the past fifteen years.

BILLY. I wouldn't say homely, exactly.

TOM. Oh yes. In fact she wrote me in her last letter that she's so homely that they make her stay in her room most of the time. Besides, they don't let you wear make-up in those convents.

FRYBURGER. I wonder what she does in her room all the time?

TOM. Oh, just sits and talks to herself in Latin, I suppose.

FRYBURGER. She speaks Latin?

TOM. Fluently.

BILLY. Fluently? She speaks Latin fluently? You didn't tell me that!

TOM. It just came to me.

FRYBURGER. She sounds like quite a girl. I never met anyone who spoke Latin.

TOM. You'll never meet anyone quite like Sister Fernando.

BILLY. You aren't kidding, brother.

FRYBURGER. It's amazing. Sometimes it takes something like a death in the family to bring people together again. I understand your father didn't get along too well with the late Mr. Buckle.

BILLY. Are you kidding? Dad was like a son to him.

FRYBURGER. To tell the truth, the whole handling of this will is very irregular. You'll leave with your inheritance in your pocket.

TOM. Is that so?

FRYBURGER. Providing you receive anything at all. If your side of the family is as hated as I hear, Lisa may be left everything.

TOM. I hadn't thought of that.

FRYBURGER. Your grandfather's maid tells me she probably won't even recognize Lisa.

BILLY. She won't recognize her, all right.

TOM. Do you think anyone else who works here might remember her enough to recognize her?

FRYBURGER. There are no servants left.

TOM. Gee, that's a shame.

FRYBURGER. Your grandfather was somewhat of a recluse in his last years. Besides an occasional nurse, Virginia was his only contact with the outside world. Why, when he and your father blew up in the bathtub...

(TOM and BILLY lower their heads in respect.)

...Virginia was the only domestic left.

Where did she run off to? Please excuse me. I'll go find Virginia so she can show you to your rooms. They're very difficult to find.

BILLY. Oh, that's okay. We know where they are.

(TOM hits him as FRYBURGER turns back.)

FRYBURGER. How would you know that? You haven't been in this house for seventeen years.

TOM. We have excellent memories of the house. Very vivid and accurate.

BILLY. He's got every inch of this house up there.

(BILLY points to TOM's head.)

FRYBURGER. That's incredible. You haven't been in this house in seventeen years.

TOM. Well, it seems more like yesterday to us.

BILLY. It seems more like this morning to me.

FRYBURGER. I'll be right back. Help yourself to a drink.

TOM. Thank you.

FRYBURGER. There are hors d'oeuvres if you're hungry.

TOM. Thank you. We've eaten.

FRYBURGER. I won't be long.

(He exits.)

TOM & BILLY. Food!

(They stuff their faces with hors d'oeuvres.)

BILLY. Boy, am I hungry. What did you do with all of our food at the apartment?

TOM. Believe it or not, I feel bad about what we're doing to Lisa. So, I made her some sandwiches and stocked a cooler of Dr. Pepper.

BILLY. Why did you leave me here last night? When I woke up this morning under that drop cloth, I thought I'd gone blind. I could have gotten caught.

TOM. You didn't get caught, did you? I had to leave last night to find a nun suit.

BILLY. Habit. They're called "habits."

TOM. What did you do, research your role?

BILLY. I wish I had. I don't know how to act like a nun. Jesus, I'm a Protestant!

TOM. Don't swear. No swearing. That's all you need to know. No swearing!

BILLY. I can't get away with this.

TOM. It's going to be a snap. Just cross yourself a lot. Just keep crossing.

> (As **TOM** munches, **BILLY** tries crossing himself – with his left hand.)

BILLY. How does it go? Right to left? Or left to right?

TOM. What's the difference?

BILLY. What's the difference? I do it wrong and I go to jail! That's the difference.

TOM. Look. Left to right is Orthodox Catholic. And right to left is regular Catholic.

BILLY. I never heard that.

TOM. That's why you're a Protestant. Trust me.

BILLY. Can't I be arrested for impersonating a nun?

TOM. That's for police. Not nuns.

BILLY. I could be struck down dead by You-Know-Who.

TOM. *(Moving away.)* Don't be silly. You'd better practice. Cross yourself and genuflect.

BILLY. Cross myself and do what?

TOM. Genuflect.

BILLY. I will not. That's disgusting!

TOM. Genuflect means...you do a little curtsy. That's very Catholic. It'll make you look real authentic. That'll really convince them.

BILLY. Yeah?

TOM. Look, you'd better practice. Just walk around and genuflect. Like this.

> (**TOM** *demonstrates. He takes three big steps and genuflects.* **BILLY** *follows and they walk around walking and genuflecting. It evolves into a combination genuflection-cha cha.*)

BILLY. I wish I was dead. Where did you say you hid my clothes?

TOM. Underneath the bed in the blue room on the third floor of the north wing.

BILLY. We're never going to get away with this. It's going to take me three days just to find the room.

TOM. Everything's worked out. You heard Mr. Fryburger say that the inheritance will be doled out right into our greedy little hands, so all we have to do is grab Lisa when she comes in and hide her there behind the bookcase. There's a secret room back there. It's very roomie. It's even got its own bathroom.

> (**BILLY** *heads for the bookcase.*)

Where are you going?

BILLY. I want a Dr. Pepper.

TOM. Get over here. Let's rehearse.

BILLY. Rehearse what?

TOM. You think kidnapping is something you just do?

> (**BILLY** *nods.*)

Look, when she comes inside, you grab her from behind and put your hands over her mouth. You'll be positioned up there on that chair.

> (**TOM** *pushes* **BILLY** *into place on a chair to the right of the arch.*)

BILLY. Why do we have to stand on chairs?

TOM. For an element of surprise. Now, when she comes in, you grab her and I'll tie her up.

BILLY. With what? You haven't got any rope.

TOM. It's in the suitcase. Then, I'll gag her.

BILLY. With what? You haven't got a gag.

TOM. It's in the suitcase. Then we take a needle of novacaine and stick her legs with it, so she can't escape.

BILLY. You should get her in the mouth too, so she can't scream.

TOM. Yeah, that's a great idea. Then we stick her in the wall. Then you go get dressed. It's a snap.

BILLY. Did you get the novacaine?

TOM & BILLY. It's in the suitcase.

> (**TOM** *opens suitcase and hands* **BILLY** *a huge needle. During the following, he takes out two pieces of rope and a gag and positions them on the back of the sofa for easy reaching.*)

BILLY. What was grandfather doing with novacaine?

TOM. He was working on painless belt buckles for fat people.

BILLY. What do we do about Fryburger and Virginia? They're not just gonna stand around and let us get away with our little scheme.

TOM. Fryburger? We simply tell him that he's wanted back at his office for some emergency. With him out of the house, we'll never be detected.

BILLY. Virginia might see us.

TOM. She's busy draining the wine cellar dry. She'll never see us. Let's get moving. We haven't got much time. Lisa's going to be here in exactly ten minutes.

BILLY. How did you know that?

TOM. I had a special cab waiting to meet her at the train station. He's taking an out-of-the-way short cut through Hackensack.

BILLY. Where did you get the money for cab fare?

TOM. I pawned your dog.

BILLY. What?

TOM. Look Billy, listen to me. You'll get your dog back. Lisa is not going to be hurt. No one is going to suspect us of anything. Afterwards we can explain everything to Lisa and I'm sure she will understand. She's going to be quite comfortable. She isn't going to lose a nickel of her inheritance. After the race tomorrow, we can come back and let her out.

BILLY. I hope she's got a sense of humor.

(Offstage we hear **FRYBURGER** *calling: "Virginia!")*

TOM. Here comes Fryburger! Hide the novacaine. Into action!

BILLY. What?

TOM. Hide that needle!

*(***BILLY** *hides it in his back pocket, covering it with his jacket.)*

Go pretend to talk on the phone with his office.

BILLY. I don't want to. I'm afraid.

TOM. Will you do it!

BILLY. What do I say?

TOM. It's a cinch. Just say, "What? An emergency at the office? We'll send Mr. Fryburger right over." And then hang up.

BILLY. Why don't you do it?

TOM. You have a much better telephone voice than I do. Hurry up. Here he comes!

(He drags **BILLY** *to the phone and forces him to sit at it.)*

TOM. Now calm down!

BILLY. Oooh!

TOM. What's the matter?

BILLY. Uh...nothing.

TOM. Relax, you look strange. Pick up the receiver!

> (**BILLY** *quickly puts the receiver to his ear and* **FRYBURGER** *enters.*)

FRYBURGER. I can't find that woman anywhere.

BILLY. "What? An emergency at the office and I should send Mr. Fryburger over immediately right away?"

FRYBURGER. Oh, is that for me?

> (**FRYBURGER** *starts for the phone and* **BILLY** *hangs it up.*)

BILLY. They hung up.

FRYBURGER. What was all that about?

> (**BILLY** *shrugs.*)

TOM. There seems to be an emergency at your office. You're supposed to leave and hurry over there immediately.

FRYBURGER. What kind of emergency?

> (**BILLY** *shrugs to himself.*)

TOM. Uh...what kind of emergency is it, Billy?

BILLY. Huh?

TOM. (*Calmly passing the buck.*) What kind of emergency is it?

BILLY. (*Panicked.*) What kind of emergency is it?

FRYBURGER. Maybe I should call them back.

TOM & BILLY. No!

BILLY. There's no time. You're supposed to go to the train station and pick up Cousin Lisa. She doesn't know how to get out here.

> (**BILLY** *shrugs back to* **TOM.**)

FRYBURGER. Oh. I'd better get right over there. How will I know her?

BILLY. You can't miss her. She looks just like a nun.

FRYBURGER. I suppose so. I'll be as quick as I can.

TOM. Fine, but take your time.

(TOM escorts FRYBURGER out quickly.)

Good thinking, Billy. Now, she'll be here any second. Places! We'd better run through this again.

BILLY. I can't.

TOM. Of course you can. Get up on your chair.

BILLY. I can't.

TOM. Of course you can. Hurry up and get up on your chair.

BILLY. I can't get up.

TOM. You aren't chickening out now.

(TOM pulls BILLY to his feet. He wobbles to the floor with rubber legs. TOM panics.)

What's the matter with you?

BILLY. I sat on the needle.

(BILLY pulls out bent needle.)

TOM. You sat on the novacaine?

BILLY. I sat on the novacaine.

TOM. You idiot!

(He drops BILLY, who falls. TOM begins pacing.)

That's the only novacaine I could find up there! Now go upstairs and find some more.

BILLY. How can I go upstairs if I can't get out of the chair?

TOM. Great! That's just great. How am I supposed to knock her out without any novacaine? How am I supposed to tie her up and gag her all by myself?

BILLY. *(Crying.)* You told me to hide the needle.

TOM. Now don't start crying. All right. I've got it. You lay on the floor. Pretend you're dead. And when she bends down to take your pulse, I'll knock her out with this vase. Then I can tie her up and it'll be a piece of cake.

BILLY. I don't want to lay on the floor. It's all dirty.

TOM. What about if she gives you mouth to mouth resuscitation?

BILLY. Now you're talking.

(**TOM** *lowers him to the floor.*)

TOM. We're all set. Now, look dead.

BILLY. How do I look dead?

TOM. Bug out your eyes and stiffen your legs.

(**TOM** *tries stiffening* **BILLY**'s *legs. They wobble around.*)

BILLY. Okay.

(*He bugs his eyes out.*)

Are they stiff?

TOM. No. Now stiffen your legs.

(**TOM** *tries again,* **BILLY**'s *legs just wobble around.*)

BILLY. Okay. Are they stiff now?

TOM. No. Look, just bug your eyes out. Maybe she won't look at your legs.

(*Doorbell.*)

Here she is. Places!

(**TOM** *gets up on his chair and waits.*)

BILLY. (*After waiting a beat with his eyes bugging out.*) Who's going to answer the door?

TOM. What do you mean?

BILLY. She's not going to come in, if no one answers the door.

TOM. I forgot about the door.

BILLY. Great plan.

TOM. All right. I'll get the door. You stay where you are.

(**TOM** *exits out the archway.* **BILLY** *poses dead with his eyes shut as* **VIRGINIA** *enters from the cellar.*)

VIRGINIA. I thought I heard the door. Billy, did you hear the door? What are you doing down there? Billy? What are you, dead or something?

(She feels his pulse and drops his arm.)

He is dead!

*(**BILLY**'s eyes bug out in surprise, as **VIRGINIA** gets an idea and begins to make eyes behind his back.)*

I'd better give you the kiss of life.

*(She smothers him with a long kiss. **BILLY**'s arms flail, smack himself in the head and pound the floor. Finally **VIRGINIA** pulls away.)*

Are you all right, now?

BILLY. I'm going to be sick to my stomach.

VIRGINIA. I saved your life. I hope you'll remember me in your will.

BILLY. I don't think I'll ever forget you.

*(**BILLY** spits.)*

VIRGINIA. Well, if you'd care to join me, I'll be in the wine cellar.

(She flirtatiously exits back into cellar.)

BILLY. *(Spitting.)* I wish I was dead.

*(**TOM** races in. **BILLY** continues spitting.)*

TOM. Well, I hope you're happy now.

BILLY. Not particularly, no.

TOM. She's got a baby.

BILLY. What?

TOM. She's got a baby with her. Who would have thought she'd have a baby?

BILLY. Great. Now we'll need two vases.

TOM. We're not going to tie up the baby, you jackass! We'll have to hide the kid somewhere. I told her I heard a scream. Now, pretend to be dead and when she comes in here, I'll knock her out.

BILLY. Is she pretty? I'm not going to be kissed by two ugly women in a row.

TOM. Shut up and be dead. Here she comes.

> (**BILLY** *plays dead, as* **TOM** *strikes a grieving pose. A beautiful blonde* **GIRL** *in her mid-twenties enters with a totally blanketed baby. She looks worried.* **TOM** *plays up his grief.*)

GIRL. I didn't hear anyone scream. There's no one in the dining hall.

TOM. *(Posing.)* Look! It's my brother Billy! I think he's dead. I've felt his pulse and it's fading fast.

GIRL. What should we do?

TOM. Give him the kiss of life and I'll call for an ambulance.

GIRL. Oh, all right.

> (*She hands her baby to* **TOM.**)

But I don't know how. What do I do?

TOM. You lean over him and kiss him. As long and as passionately as you possibly can.

> (**BILLY** *peeks and rubs his hands with glee after seeing the* **GIRL.**)

We've got to get his heart going.

> (**BILLY** *poses "dead" but with his lips puckered and ready to go.*)

His life depends on it.

GIRL. Well, all right. I'll get his heart going.

> (**TOM** *gets the vase, juggling the baby in the other arm.*)

TOM. Not racing. Just get it going.

GIRL. I hope I do this right. I've never saved anyone's life before.

> (*The* **GIRL** *gets within fractions of an inch to kissing* **BILLY.**)

TOM. Forget it. I can't do it. Forget it.

GIRL. Were we too late?

(She takes his pulse as **TOM** *sets the vase back down.)*

Oh! He is dead!

*(***BILLY*** looks surprised.)*

TOM. I can't go through with it. He isn't really dead.

BILLY. Yes, I am! I am so dead!

(He assumes puckered dead position as the **GIRL** *squeals.)*

TOM. She's got a baby! I can't strike a woman.

BILLY. You can so. Remember Debbie Ciardello?

TOM. That was different. We didn't know you had a baby.

GIRL. I don't even know you.

TOM. I'm Tom and that's Billy. It's been quite a while. Now listen, a man is coming here to kill my brother and myself. We need your help.

BILLY. We're still going through with this?

TOM. We have to.

GIRL. Going through with what? What are you talking about?

BILLY. I don't think we should.

TOM. Billy, sit up so you can help me.

*(***BILLY*** sits up positioning his rubber legs into a sitting position.)*

BILLY. You see, I'm supposed to be a nun. I can't have a child. What would people say?

GIRL. Who are you? You're supposed to be a nun? You're crazy!

BILLY. At first that's what I thought. But you should see me in my robe.

GIRL. What man wants to kill you?

BILLY. A mobster. We're desperate. Please help us.

GIRL. Of course. What can I do?

TOM. *(Handing baby to* **BILLY.***)* Cross your arms. Across your chest.

BILLY. If you can.

> (**TOM** *retrieves a piece of rope from the sofa.*)

TOM. Would you hold this please?

> (*The* **GIRL** *holds the rope as* **TOM** *begins to tie her up with her help.*)

BILLY. What a cute little baby.

GIRL. What are you doing? Are you practicing for the man who's coming to kill you? Are you practicing tying him up?

TOM. Exactly. What do you think? Would this way work?

> (**TOM** *completes tying her feet.*)

GIRL. Oh, definitely. Don't forget to gag him. As long as he could talk he could always scream for help.

TOM. I hadn't thought of that.

GIRL. Do you have a handkerchief or something?

TOM. Here. How about this one?

> (*He holds up pre-planned gag.*)

GIRL. That would be good.

TOM. Open wide.

> (*The* **GIRL** *opens her mouth wide, but* **BILLY** *interrupts them.*)

BILLY. Hey! I got the feeling back in my legs!

TOM. Forgive Billy. He's been a semi-invalid for years. War wound.

GIRL. Poor thing.

TOM. Open wide.

> (*She does and is gagged.*)

Now does that hurt you at all?

> (*She shakes her head "no."*)

Can you scream?

> (*She shakes her head.*)

Are you totally helpless?

(She nods.)

BILLY. *(On his knees.)* You'd better hurry up. Fryburger's going to be back here any second.

TOM. Well, I didn't count on a baby. And you sitting on the novacaine. It's taken a little longer than I expected.

(TOM heads for the bookcase, looking for a secret lever.)

BILLY. *(To GIRL.)* I hope you find this all amusing tomorrow. We're really nice guys and normally we wouldn't harm a fly. We wouldn't even be doing this but Tom had hot tips.

TOM. *(Frantic.)* I can't find the secret room. Where's the secret room?

BILLY. Behind the bookcase!

TOM. I know it's behind the bookcase. Help me look. You said you had the feeling back in your legs.

BILLY. Okay.

(TOM returns to the bookcase in search of the secret passage, as BILLY attempts to stand up, baby in arms.)

Hey look, I can stand up.

(BILLY's legs give out and he falls to the floor. The baby flies through the air and TOM turns just in time to catch him. The GIRL screams under her gag.)

TOM. What's the matter with you?

BILLY. I slipped. I'm sorry I slipped.

(BILLY takes the baby and goes up to the GIRL.)

I slipped.

(The GIRL screams.)

I don't think Lisa's too happy about this, are you?

(She screams again.)

(Setting baby down on the tea cart.)

Rockabye baby on the tea cart…

TOM. Reassure her! Will you reassure her!

>(**BILLY** *approaches the* **GIRL**.)

BILLY. You're a very pretty lady.

>(*She screams again.*)

TOM. Forget the secret room. We'll put her in the closet. Now, grab her and follow me. Hurry up.

>(**TOM** *heads for the closet.*)

BILLY. What?

I said, grab her and follow me.

>(**BILLY** *grabs her ass and follows* **TOM** *into the closet.*)

What are you doing?

BILLY. I'm following you.

TOM. Didn't I tell you to grab her?

BILLY. I did.

TOM. Bring her with you!

BILLY. Oh, well, how am I supposed to know?!

TOM. I'll make sure everything is comfortable.

>(**TOM** *pushes aside hangers and sets her bag inside closet. He turns back to see* **BILLY** *extending an arm to the* **GIRL**. *She shakes her head. He holds his arms out for her to jump in, motioning with his head. She shakes her head "no" again.*)

What are you doing?

BILLY. You know about my problem.

TOM. Will you hurry up!

>(**BILLY** *tries lifting her straight up. His face falls into her cleavage. His shoes rise but he and the* **GIRL** *do not.*)

Over your shoulder, Billy. Put her over your shoulder.

BILLY. Fireman carry. Fireman Carry!

(He lifts her up and does a take to her perfect ass.)

How about if I stay in the closet to make sure she doesn't escape?

TOM. It's bad enough we're going to be arrested for kidnapping. We don't need attempted rape on the list.

*(The baby cries. **TOM** quickly shuts the closet door with **BILLY** and the **GIRL** inside. He tries to shut the baby up by rocking it on the tea cart.)*

Rockabye baby on the tea cart...

*(To silence the baby, he lifts the dome lid and sets it on the tray, covering the kid. The cry stops. From the cellar, **VIRGINIA** enters. **TOM** hastily grabs a book off the bookcase and begins reading. The book is upside down.)*

VIRGINIA. What are you up to, Mr. Buckle?

TOM. Reading, Virginia. I love to read. I could read all day long sometimes. Yessir. Sometimes I just sit and read for hours on end.

VIRGINIA. It'd probably take you less time if you read it right side up.

TOM. Huh? Oh. It's a Chinese book. In China they read upside down.

VIRGINIA. That sounds very odd to me.

TOM. Actually what I meant to say is... I have dyslexia. Yes, that's much better. I'm ashamed of it. I don't tell too many people, but you have a face I can trust....

VIRGINIA. Mr. Buckle, I don't care what you're doing with that book. If you're looking for the booze, I hide it behind the Dickens. It's good stuff, too. You could knock a girl unconscious. Get her so loaded, she couldn't walk. *(Winks.)* You get me?

TOM. *(Looking to closet.)* Yes, I do get you.

(Doorbell.)

It would be kinder than novacaine anyway.

VIRGINIA. You could look at it that way. If you'll pardon me, I'll go get dinner started.

> (**VIRGINIA** *wheels off the tea cart, along with the baby, but it doesn't register with* **TOM**, *who is more concerned with the closet. He rushes to it, finding the hidden booze along the way. An irate* **BILLY** *pops out of the closet and the door is slammed shut.*)

BILLY. Who do you think you're pushing, buster?

TOM. Virginia came in. Is everything all right?

BILLY. I think I'm in love. From the way she fell on me, I think we have to get married.

TOM. We don't have time for that. I want you to do something. Get her drunk. It'll make everything much easier.

BILLY. I don't think I need to get her drunk. She goes for me, man, she goes for me.

> (**JANE** *enters, unnoticed.* **JANE** *is a beautiful brunette, smartly dressed. She stops short and eavesdrops, unseen by the boys.*)

TOM. Listen, you jackass, we've got to keep Lisa in that closet. If we can't stick her with novacaine to keep her in there, we've got to use something else. So, we'll get her drunk and hope she passes out.

> (**TOM** *opens closet and shoves bottle inside.*)

Here. Drink this!

> (*He slams door shut again.*)

BILLY. I've been explaining our plan to her. I think she understands what's going on.

TOM. What have you told her?

BILLY. I told her we were in debt to a mobster and needed to borrow her inheritance money to pay him off. I told her we'd pay her back.

TOM. What'd she say?

(**BILLY** *whispers in* **TOM**'s *ear.* **TOM** *slaps him.*)

What else did you tell her?

BILLY. I told her I'd be impersonating her, so she'd have to stay in the closet until tomorrow. Oh, I took the gag out. I felt it was unkind.

TOM. She can speak?

BILLY. Sure she can speak. And what a sexy voice. She said the dirtiest things to me.

TOM. I'll bet. She better keep her mouth shut. If Fryburger finds out that Lisa isn't a nun, we're in a lot of hot water.

(**JANE** *backs out of the room, unnoticed.*)

BILLY. She wants her baby. Please, let's at least give her her baby back. You're not supposed to separate a mother and a child at such an early age or they don't let them back into the nest.

TOM. We can take care of the baby ourselves. We can't have it crying in the wall. It'll give everything away.

BILLY. On top of everything else we've got to do, we've got to watch a baby? Who's going to feed it?

TOM. You can feed it.

BILLY. *(Indicating his chest.)* With what?

TOM. Oh. Okay, we'll give the baby back. But she better keep her mouth shut in there.

BILLY. Okay, hurry up. Where's the baby?

TOM. Right over... I put the kid...

BILLY. Where's the baby?

TOM. Don't you have him?

BILLY. No! I thought you had him!

(*They frantically search the room.*)

TOM. I know he's here somewhere. Don't just stand there. Look for him.

BILLY. Here boy! Here boy! How could you lose a baby?

(*Doorbell.*)

TOM. Who is that?

BILLY. What am I? The Man With the X-Ray Eyes or something? How should I know who it is?

TOM. Find that baby!

(VIRGINIA enters with JANE.)

VIRGINIA. Gentlemen...

(TOM and BILLY look behind them.)

This is...what's the name?

JANE. Jane Doemaker. Jane Doemaker. I was your grandfather's nurse a long time ago. Is this where they're reading the will?

BILLY. Yes, hi there, I'm...

(TOM pulls him back and introduces himself.)

TOM. How do you do, Miss Doemaker.

(Kisses her hand and is in love.)

I'm Thomas T. Buckle. I wasn't aware grandfather had a nurse.

VIRGINIA. Me neither. I'm never going to get anything out of this will.

(We see an instant attraction between TOM and JANE. BILLY feels left out.)

JANE. It's been quite a while since I worked for Mr. Buckle. When he used to vacation in Miami I'd always go along and look after him. We'd go to the beach and I'd rotate him.

(BILLY and TOM react.)

VIRGINIA. Mr. Buckle liked having beauty all around him. Nurses, cooks, masseuses, maids...even his mechanic was a woman. So, you were one of those nurses, huh?

JANE. I give a great sponge bath.

TOM. I could use a cold shower.

JANE. I beg your pardon?

TOM. I said, "Look at the hour." It's almost five o'clock.

(**VIRGINIA** *has been looking* **JANE** *up and down. She pushes her bust up to see if it is as firm as* **JANE**'s. *It isn't.*)

VIRGINIA. I'll go start dinner.

(She exits mumbling to herself.)

I bet she pads.

TOM. My, my, look at the time. Billy, why don't you go see what's keeping our dear cousin Lisa.

BILLY. I want to talk to the nurse.

TOM. Billy, I really think you should go see what's keeping our dear cousin. *(To* **JANE**.*)* Our dear cousin Lisa...she arrived a short while ago from her convent. Far, far away.

JANE. *(Glancing to closet.)* Convent?

TOM. Yes. Our dear cousin Lisa has become a nun. Sister Angelica Agnes Catherine Fernando Bertrille.

JANE. What a pretty name.

BILLY. Thank you.

JANE. So, your cousin's a nun. Are there any more relatives?

TOM. No, just us. Billy and I are brothers and Lisa's a distant relative.

JANE. I'll bet she's a lot closer than you let on.

TOM. Well, in a way. Billy, go see what's keeping Sister Fernando.

BILLY. Can't it wait a while? I have to work up my nerve.

JANE. Work up your nerve for what?

TOM. Billy gets tongue-tied speaking to nuns. It reminds him of his sinful youth. If you look at his hands he still has ruler marks. Get going before we have to go downtown and make a confession.

BILLY. I'll be right back! No, I mean Sister Fernando will be right back. Tom, while I'm gone, see if you can locate that missing item.

TOM. *(Having forgotten.)* What item?

(Unseen by **JANE**, **BILLY** *cradles his arms.)*

BILLY. You remember.

> (**JANE** *turns in time to catch the end of his pantomime. He pretends to be cold.*)

Cold in here. Brrr. Boy, is it cold in here. See if you can find that sweater of mine, Tom.

TOM. Sweater, right. Billy's been ill lately. Where'd we put that?

JANE. It's a good thing I'm a nurse. Come here, you poor thing. How can you be so cold? It's so hot in here. Are you running a temperature?

> (*She holds* **BILLY**'s *head. Then places a finger under his nose.*)

BILLY. Isn't this for dogs?

JANE. You don't seem ill.

TOM. It comes and goes. He runs hot and cold. Run upstairs and lie down.

BILLY. (*Loading up the suitcases.*) Good idea. It was nice meeting you. Be careful where you sit.

> (**BILLY** *races up the stairs to change.*)

JANE. I will. What did that mean? "Be careful where I sit"?

TOM. We wouldn't want you to sit in a draft and catch his disease.

> (**TOM** *continues searching for the baby.*)

JANE. That's very thoughtful. Can I help you look?

TOM. No! I mean, it's such an old sweater. Who cares where it is.

> (**JANE** *sits on the sofa.* **TOM** *tenses and follows her all the way down, to make sure she doesn't sit on the baby. He sighs.*)

Comfortable, isn't it?

> (**FRYBURGER** *enters. He is disheveled. He walks doubled over. He slams his briefcase down.*)

Mr. Fryburger! What happened to you?

FRYBURGER. I sat at that train station for one hour. I kept paging her and she never came. So, I went walking around the track and...there she was. I saw her standing in a line for the ladies room. So, I went up to her.

TOM. How did you know it was her?

FRYBURGER. She was exactly the way you described her. Boy, was she ugly!

TOM. You really found Sister Fernando.

FRYBURGER. I thought I had. I told her who I was. And I tried to get her into my car.

TOM. What happened?

FRYBURGER. She kicked me between the legs and two policemen threw me up against a wall.

TOM. Gee, that's a shame. Sister Fernando arrived right after you left.

FRYBURGER. What?

TOM. How'd you get out of it?

FRYBURGER. I made a large donation to her church. But it's all right. It's a tax write-off.

TOM. Mr. Fryburger, I'd like you to meet Jane Doemaker. She was one of grandfather's nurses. A long time ago.

FRYBURGER. How long ago? You must have been in diapers.

JANE. One of us was. How do you do, Mr. Fryburger. I thought I'd just show up. You never know who's going to be remembered and who isn't.

TOM. I can guess who isn't.

*(**FRYBURGER** kisses her hand and a lecherous glint appears in his eye.)*

FRYBURGER. How lovely to meet you, Miss Doemaker. I always appreciate a beautiful woman.

*(Behind their backs, **BILLY** enters down the staircase as **SISTER FERNANDO**. He wears a traditional habit, complete with starched bib and wimple. He reluctantly descends the stairs as **TOM** waves him on.)*

TOM. Sister Fernando! Look everybody! It's Sister Fernando!

(**FRYBURGER** *and* **JANE** *turn to greet* **SISTER FERNANDO.**)

FRYBURGER. Well, how nice to meet you, Sister.

(**BILLY** *walks and genuflects to everyone.*)

BILLY. Hello, my son. Hello, my daughter. Hello, my brother.

(**TOM** *reacts with horror at* **BILLY**'s *behavior.*)

FRYBURGER. I'm Robert Fryburger. You're exactly how your cousin described you. I hope you had a pleasant trip up.

BILLY. Yes. But it's hot in this thing. What I'd give for cut-offs and a t-shirt.

FRYBURGER. It's funny. I haven't seen a nun dressed in that type of habit for a very long time.

BILLY. Well, old habits are hard to break.

FRYBURGER. Yes. Well. I'd like you to meet Jane Doemaker. Your grandfather's nurse.

BILLY. *(Genuflecting.)* Hello, my daughter.

FRYBURGER. Miss Doemaker, this is Sister Fernando.

(**JANE** *extends a hand, but* **BILLY** *genuflects.* **JANE**, *in turn, curtsies. Business of alternate "curtsying" until* **BILLY** *waves it off.*)

JANE. Pleased to meet you. I always wanted to meet Mr. Buckle's granddaughter. He was so proud of you belonging to the church.

(**TOM** *and* **BILLY** *react.*)

BILLY. He was? That's impossible.

JANE. Why is that?

BILLY. ...Grandfather was an atheist.

JANE. Tell me. How do they pick a nun's new name? I understand that when you enter the church you leave behind your past and receive a new name.

BILLY. Oh, we just pick it out of a hat.

> (**TOM** *is dying.*)

FRYBURGER. Tom told us that you speak Latin fluently.

BILLY. Big mouth.

JANE. Would you say something in Latin for us?

BILLY. Well...

JANE & FRYBURGER. Please???

> (**BILLY** *gives in and steps forward to say something. All eyes are on him. He cannot think of a thing in Latin. Finally...*)

BILLY. E Pluribus Unum. To you all.

> (**TOM** *nervously laughs.* **JANE** *and* **FRYBURGER** *politely laugh at what they suppose was a joke.* **BILLY** *laughs too, nervously.*)

FRYBURGER. What a sense of humor. Tell, me, what convent do you belong to?

> (*He opens a notepad and prepares to write.*)

BILLY. It's a new one. The Convent of the...Sisters...of Brotherly Love.

JANE. Where is that, Philadelphia?

BILLY. No, it's far away. In fact, you can't get there from here.

> (**VIRGINIA** *wheels in the same tea cart, and same dome-lidded tray.*)

VIRGINIA. Dinner is served in one hour. Eat these appetizer things for now.

FRYBURGER. Virginia, here's little Lisa.

VIRGINIA. That's Lisa? Oh, and you were such a beautiful child.

FRYBURGER. Forgive Virginia, Sister Fernando. She likes her wine.

BILLY. Oh, that's all right. I like a good belt now and then myself.

VIRGINIA. You better eat them finger sandwiches before they get cold. It's a good thing you decided to enter the church, Lisa. You grew up homelier than Billy did.

JANE. Would you care to say grace for us, Sister?

BILLY. Say what?

JANE. Grace? A prayer that gives thanks for the food.

BILLY. Thank you, but I'm on vacation.

TOM. What a funny nun. Go ahead, Sister.

>   (**BILLY** *waves them to bow their heads. He stands over the big tray cover.*)

BILLY. Dear God, for what we are about to receive, let us be truly thankful.

>   (**BILLY** *lifts the cover while everyone keeps their heads bowed. The baby is still under there. He slams the lid down and his eyes bulge out.*)

TOM. Psst. Amen.

BILLY. AMEN!

>   (*Everyone's eyes are startled open.*)

FRYBURGER. Well, we can eat our appetizers now and then read the will before dinner.

BILLY. No!!

TOM. What's wrong?

BILLY. It's cold in here.

>   (**BILLY** *cradles his arms but can't get through to* **TOM.**)

Boy is it cold in here.

TOM. What are you talking about? It's very warm in here. You were just saying how warm it was in here.

BILLY. Warm isn't the right word. Hot is the word. Hot. Hot.

>   (**TOM** *catches on.*)

FRYBURGER. You just said it was cold.

TOM. That's Latin for hot. Cold means hot in Latin.

FRYBURGER. Cold means hot?

TOM. It comes from the Latin...coldus hottum.

FRYBURGER. I didn't know that.

JANE. Well, shall we eat? I'm starved.

TOM & BILLY. No!!!

TOM. We can't eat without Billy. That would be rude.

FRYBURGER. Where is Billy?

JANE. Upstairs lying down. I'll go get him.

TOM & BILLY. NO!!!

TOM. Let Sister Fernando go get him. She can use the exercise. And besides, everyone knows the air is cooler up there.

FRYBURGER. *(Rises.)* Hot air rises.

BILLY. Don't get up. I won't be but a minute. Don't eat anything until we get back!

(**BILLY** *dashes up the stairs.*)

FRYBURGER. What a strange woman.

VIRGINIA. Lisa was a beautiful child. With a little...button nose. What happened to her?

TOM. Maybe she was in a car wreck. Did you ever think of that? If you noticed, she has a slight limp. I'll bet my money it was a car wreck.

FRYBURGER. I should check out her credentials anyway. Let me go phone my office. I'll put a call out to the Convent of the Sisters of Brotherly Love and see if there is a Sister Fernando there. I'll use the upstairs phone. Excuse me.

(**FRYBURGER** *exits with* **VIRGINIA** *close behind.*)

VIRGINIA. *(Exiting.)* There's a phone in my room, Bob.

TOM. What's the big fuss? So she grew up ugly? Is that any reason for an investigation?

JANE. You never know who'd try to commit fraud. Maybe this isn't your cousin at all. Just a run of the mill nun looking for a big donation.

TOM. How can you say that? That's my cousin.

JANE. You haven't seen her in seventeen years. How do you know?

TOM. I'd know my own cousin. Why does everyone doubt me?

JANE. I have no idea. You have such an honest face.

> (**BILLY** *dashes in as* **BILLY**. *His hair is a mess, his tie is loose.*)

BILLY. Yes? You were looking for me?

JANE. How are you feeling now?

BILLY. Great.

JANE. Where's Sister Fernando?

BILLY. Now she's lying down.

TOM. Mr. Fryburger is putting a call out to the Convent of the Sisters of Brotherly Love.

BILLY. What?

JANE. He just wants to make sure she really is your Cousin Lisa. He just needs a little evidence. One phone call should clear it all up. I'll go see how he's doing.

> (**JANE** *exits after* **FRYBURGER**.)

BILLY. *(Calling.)* The number may not be listed!

TOM. You jackass! Get that girl out of there and give her her baby back. We've got some quick explaining to do. Or we are going to jail. I hope she cooperates.

BILLY. She will. She's crazy about me.

> (**BILLY** *gets the baby from under the dome.*)

Great plan you thought of. What are we going to say when they find out there isn't any Convent of the Sisters of Brotherly Love? They'll know you were lying all the time.

TOM. Me "lying"? Me? I never said what convent she belonged to. You're the liar. Thanks to you we're both in trouble.

BILLY. Thanks to me?

TOM. Yes, you. *(Imitates him.)* "E Pluribus Unum." If you'd been convincing enough they wouldn't have to check out anything. Would you get rid of that baby!

BILLY. *(Crying.)* I didn't want to do this in the first place. I told you I wouldn't know how to act like a nun. Hey! How did that nurse know Lisa was a nun anyway? How could she have known Lisa was a nun if Lisa wasn't a nun until today?

TOM. I haven't any idea. All I do know is that in about ten minutes they'll know she isn't a nun and you'll have a lot of explaining to do.

BILLY. Me?

> (**JANE** *re-enters.*)

TOM. Would you hide that.

> (**BILLY** *hides the baby behind his back.* **TOM** *forces* **JANE** *to keep from turning to* **BILLY**, *who tries to open the closet and get rid of the baby. It is pulled shut from inside. He knocks, she won't open it up. He tries pulling it open, it is locked from the inside.* **BILLY** *tries hiding the baby in drawers, under cushions...he can't find a place at all.*)

Why, hello Jane. We were just talking about you.

JANE. Saying good things I hope.

TOM. How could we say anything bad about you.

JANE. Mr. Fryburger isn't having any luck. He's very new at being a lawyer. He's a little over-anxious to do well. Oh, Billy...

> (As **JANE** *turns to face* **BILLY**, *in a panic*, **BILLY** *throws the baby in the air to* **TOM.** **JANE** *never sees the child.* **TOM** *catches the baby as* **BILLY** *nonchalantly poses to face* **JANE.**)

Where is Sister Fernando? You'd better get her down here so she can straighten all of this out. Don't you agree, Tom?

> (**JANE** *turns to* **TOM**, *who tosses the kid over her head back to* **BILLY**. **TOM** *nonchalantly poses to talk to* **JANE**, *as* **BILLY** *catches the baby behind her back.*)

TOM. Right. Absolutely right. Tell you what. You wait here. And I'll go get her.

> (**BILLY** *tosses the baby back as* **JANE** *turns on his voice.* **TOM** *catches the child, barely, and* **BILLY** *tries to compose himself arid speak at the same time.*)

BILLY. NNOOO!!! I mean…how are you going to go get her?

JANE. I can go get her…

TOM. (*Tossing the baby back as* **JANE** *turns to him.*) No!!! I mean, we wouldn't want you to tire yourself out going up and down those stairs.

> (**BILLY** *holds the baby up behind* **JANE**'s *back and motions with it like a quarterback trying to find an open man to pass to.*)

JANE. That's true. You never know when I'll need my strength.

TOM. Billy can go. Right now!

> (**JANE** *turns quicker than expected and* **BILLY** *hides the baby under his suit jacket. He quickly exits so* **JANE** *cannot see the baby.*)

BILLY. Well…okay. While I'm gone, why don't you ask Jane, here, about what we were discussing. I'll be right back. But first I think I'll change my clothes.

> (**BILLY** *exits upstairs and we hear the baby cry.*)

JANE. What was that?

TOM. What?

JANE. I heard a baby crying.

TOM. Oh, that? That was Billy. Whenever he changes his clothes, he cries like a baby.

JANE. Oh.

TOM. Miss Doemaker, we were wondering. If no one has seen Lisa in seventeen years, how did you know she was a nun?

JANE. Why, I told you. Mr. Buckle knew. He spoke with her all the time. He was very proud of her.

TOM. She really is a nun?

JANE. Oh yes. Has been for years.

TOM. Then who the hell...

JANE. He said the only thing that upset her about becoming a nun was having to hide her beautiful brown hair under that wimple.

TOM. Well, I can understand...brown hair? Lisa has brown hair?

JANE. Brown. Yes. Don't worry, Tom. We all know that Sister Fernando is your cousin Lisa. Mr. Fryburger just has to go through the formality of making sure. There's a lot of money involved here.

TOM. A brown-haired nun, huh?

JANE. Yes.

TOM. Who...was anyone else expected here today?

JANE. No. I wasn't even expected. I just showed up.

TOM. Oh boy.

JANE. What's wrong?

TOM. Nothing. It's getting hotter in here all the time.

> (**BILLY** *enters as* **SISTER FERNANDO**. *It is obvious from the bulge underneath that the child is hidden under there.* **TOM** *does a take to her "stomach."*)

BILLY. Here I am.

TOM. I've got to talk to you.

JANE. Where's Billy?

BILLY. He's lying down.

JANE. Did he change his clothes?

BILLY. Yes. All changed.

JANE. Did he stop crying?
BILLY. Well, he...

> (**BILLY** *looks surprised.*).

Oh. Oh. Oh.
JANE. What's wrong?
BILLY. Oh.
TOM. Sister Fernando, what's wrong?
BILLY. Oh. Somebody's hungry. Oh! Somebody's very hungry!
JANE. I'll go get Mr. Fryburger so we can eat.

> (*As the baby breastfeeds,* **BILLY** *cries out in pain.*)

I've never seen such acute hunger pains.
BILLY. Oh!
JANE. I'll be right back.

> (**JANE** *exits quickly.*)

TOM. What's the matter with you? Do you know we kidnapped the wrong girl?
BILLY. What? What are you talking about?
TOM. Lisa really is a nun! Lisa has brown hair, not blonde hair. Lisa wouldn't have a baby.
BILLY. (*Indicating his chest.*) Then what the hell is this?
TOM. I don't know. Give her her baby back, you jackass. We've got to get her out of here.

> (**TOM** *opens up the closet and shoves* **BILLY** *and the baby inside.*)

BILLY. Oh!
GIRL. HELP!!!!
TOM. Ssh! Ssh
GIRL. HELP!!! HELP!!!
BILLY. Ouch.
TOM. SHUT UP!

(**TOM** *slams the door shut, as* **JANE** *and* **FRYBURGER** *dash in to see what's wrong. In his haste,* **TOM** *closed* **BILLY** *inside as well.*)

FRYBURGER. What's wrong? What happened?

JANE. I just heard somebody scream.

TOM. That was just Sister Fernando.

FRYBURGER. Where is she?

TOM. She's right…she was here a minute ago.

JANE. She was screaming "help."

TOM. "Help-ING." She was screaming that she wanted another "helping." Very hungry lady.

JANE. That poor thing. She must be starving.

FRYBURGER. Where is she?

TOM. Where is she? She went into the wine cellar.

FRYBURGER. Why?

TOM. Why? Trying to find Virginia.

FRYBURGER. Well, that's where she'll be. Come on Jane, let's go get them so Sister Fernando can eat.

TOM. Did you get through to the convent, Mr. Fryburger?

FRYBURGER. No one's ever heard of such a convent. My office is working on it and they'll call us as soon as they hear anything.

(**FRYBURGER** *and* **JANE** *disappear into the cellar.*)

(**TOM** *opens the closet and yanks out* **BILLY**.)

TOM. What were you doing in there?

BILLY. I've got a date for Saturday night.

TOM. Did you find out who she was?

BILLY. Who had time?

TOM. Well, at least we got that baby out of the way.

(*We hear the baby crying through the wall.*)

BILLY. What's that?

TOM. QUIET IN THERE!!!

(BILLY slaps at TOM.)

BILLY. Don't you talk to my girl like that.

TOM. Great. How are we going to explain a baby crying in the closet and a girl who's not a nun screaming?

BILLY. I'm sure you'll think of something.

(FRYBURGER and JANE return with VIRGINIA.)

FRYBURGER. We found Virginia, but we couldn't find Sister Fernando.

BILLY. *(Genuflecting.)* I'm right here, my son.

FRYBURGER. How did we miss you?

BILLY. I missed you too. Welcome back.

JANE. We can eat now. We're all here except Billy.

BILLY. Thank you, but I'm not hungry.

(TOM smacks him.)

JANE. You're not hungry?

BILLY. And either is Billy!

FRYBURGER. I thought you were screaming for another helping.

(TOM nods.)

BILLY. That's true. But as much as I'd like to… I'm afraid I can't eat. Lent.

FRYBURGER. This isn't Lent.

BILLY. I'm rehearsing.

FRYBURGER. Sister Fernando, I'm trying to locate the Convent of the Sisters of Brotherly Love. Where did you say it was?

BILLY. I didn't.

FRYBURGER. I'm afraid I must call them to clarify who you are. You must agree. No one has seen you in seventeen years.

BILLY. Oh. Of course. But you see…we don't have a telephone at that convent.

FRYBURGER. Oh, you don't.

(Telephone rings.)

Excuse me, that must be my office.

> *(**FRYBURGER** answers the phone as **BILLY** and **TOM** prepare for their doom.)*

Hello. Buckle residence. Who? Just a minute. Sister Fernando, it's for you.

> *(**BILLY** and **TOM** exchange looks of confusion.)*

TOM. That's impossible. I mean…nobody knew she was here.

BILLY. Who…who is it?

FRYBURGER. It's your Mother Superior.

> *(**TOM** and **BILLY** freeze.)*

BILLY. Holy shit!!!!

> *(Curtain.)*

End of Act One

ACT II

(Seconds later, **FRYBURGER** *holds the telephone out. All eyes go to* **SISTER FERNANDO,** *who edges to the phone.)*

BILLY. Who did you say it was?

FRYBURGER. Your Mother Superior.

BILLY. *(Taking phone.)* Hello, Mother? Fine. I'm fine. Everything's fine. What? Okay, Mom. Goodbye.

TOM. What did she say?

BILLY. I have to be back on Monday.

FRYBURGER. Fine. Well, that just saved me a phone call. I'm sorry I doubted you, Sister Fernando.

BILLY. Oh, skip it.

FRYBURGER. Is everything all right?

BILLY. Yes! Why do you ask?

FRYBURGER. It's just that you don't act like most nuns.

BILLY. Well, I'm doing the best I can!

TOM. What a kidder. Sister really breaks them up at Bingo.

FRYBURGER. That's what I mean. You're awfully flippant for a nun.

BILLY. Flippant? Is that some sort of a crack?

TOM. Easy Sister. She gets so excited.

FRYBURGER. Exactly how long have you been a nun, Sister?

BILLY. What time is it?

TOM. It's been many years. Would anyone like a drink?

BILLY. I would. Water. A glass of water.

*(***TOM*** pours ***BILLY*** water and a drink of scotch for ***FRYBURGER***.)*

VIRGINIA. May I ask a question, Lisa?

(**VIRGINIA** *genuflects.*)

BILLY. *(Genuflecting back.)* Certainly, Virginia.

VIRGINIA. What made you decide to enter the church?

BILLY. How's that?

VIRGINIA. Why'd you become a nun?

BILLY. He made me do it.

FRYBURGER. He?

>(**TOM** *shoves a glass of water into* **BILLY***'s hand.*)

BILLY. He... Him!

>(**BILLY** *points up.*)

One day, after I had viewed *The Sound of Music* on television, He spoke to me. Called me to the Church. Right through that television set.

FRYBURGER. Really? How peculiar.

BILLY. It was during a commercial break.

TOM. She decided to devote her life to God's work from that day forth.

VIRGINIA. I hear voices sometimes too.

JANE. How do you know so much about it, Tom?

TOM. Gee, she must have written it in one of her letters. As I said before, Sister Fernando and I have quite a correspondence going. We're very close

JANE. Funny, Billy never mentioned any of that.

FRYBURGER. That's probably because Billy can't read. Right Tom?

TOM. Yes, that's right.

FRYBURGER. You've got a very human quality. You've got something real different for a nun.

TOM. She's got something different, all right. Sister, can I ask a question?

BILLY. Why?

TOM. How's your Mother Superior doing?

BILLY. Fine. Why do you ask?

TOM. Did she say how she got this number?

BILLY. I must have given it to her before I left. Can we get on with the will reading?

> (**BILLY** *hands glass of water to* **TOM**, *who is baffled.*)

FRYBURGER. Where is Billy? He's always disappearing. We can't start until everyone is present.

JANE. I can't wait to see this.

TOM. Well… I guess you'd, better, go get him, Sister.

BILLY. *(Muttered.)* And how the hell am I supposed to do that?

TOM. What if Billy's too ill to be present?

FRYBURGER. Well, he doesn't have to be present. What's wrong with him?

JANE. I examined him and I diagnosed as much bed rest as possible.

FRYBURGER. Maybe we should go up and see how he is.

TOM & BILLY. No!

TOM. We didn't want to say it out loud but he could be contagious. We think it's a mild form of leprosy.

VIRGINIA. Leprosy?

TOM. Yes. You'd know about that, Virginia. It was a popular disease in your youth, wasn't it?

FRYBURGER. What are you trying to pull? Nobody gets leprosy anymore.

TOM. They don't?

JANE. Very rarely. Tom is misinformed, Mr. Fryburger.

BILLY. He sure is.

JANE. Billy doesn't have leprosy at all.

BILLY. Of course not.

JANE. It looked like mumps to me. We should leave him to rest.

BILLY. What do you mean, "It looked like mumps"?

JANE. I examined him. I'd diagnose it as mumps.

BILLY. You would? *(Rubs throat.)* I don't feel so good.

TOM. Good. Then why don't you go up and lie down, Sister.

FRYBURGER. And see how Billy is doing.

JANE. If he's feeling better, you might want to send him down.

TOM. Mumps or not.

VIRGINIA. Hey! I don't want to catch his mumps. What if I decide to have children?

TOM. Tell him he better come down, Sister. Tell him I said to. No one has seen him in awhile. We wouldn't want to give anything away.

FRYBURGER. Now, now. Don't be greedy. I already told you. He doesn't have to be present to get what's coming to him.

BILLY. I'll get him! I'll get him! Jesus!

(**BILLY** *exits. All eyes look to* **TOM**.)

TOM. She's always praying.

FRYBURGER. What an amazing woman. Devoted to God. Wonderful sense of humor. She's so frank.

TOM. Frank's her middle name.

FRYBURGER. She's marvelous. She speaks Latin…

TOM. Easy. She's taken.

(**TOM** *lifts phone and listens. He hangs up.*)

FRYBURGER. What are you doing?

TOM. Oh. Just checking.

FRYBURGER. Checking for what?

TOM. Uh…sometimes rats get into these old houses and they eat the phone cords.

FRYBURGER. Rats eat the phone cords? What are you talking about?

TOM. Nope. No rats here. Where is that boy?

(**BILLY** *dashes in, hair messed up, tie loose, shirt tail out.*)

BILLY. Well, here I am.

TOM. My God, you look ill. You'd better go up and lie down.

BILLY. I just got here!

TOM. I know, but we want to get this will reading over with. You'd better go up and lie down.

BILLY. I don't think I'm up to it at the moment. I have mumps, you know.

FRYBURGER. He looks fine to me.

JANE. I'll help you upstairs, Billy.

TOM. You wouldn't want to catch his disease.

JANE. Oh, that's right.

TOM. You'd better rest. We do want you to keep up a good appearance.

BILLY. All right.

(**BILLY** *starts the long trek up the stairs. This is exhausting him.*)

TOM. Oh, if you pass Sister Fernando on the stairs, see if she can speed it up. I want to talk to her about her Mother Superior.

BILLY. *(Glaring.)* It takes her awhile. Her room is so far away.

JANE. She shouldn't have to walk down that long corridor. She can room with me. That is, if she doesn't mind sharing the bed.

BILLY. Hell no.

FRYBURGER. Could we get on with this?

TOM. Billy, go rest your mumps!

(**BILLY** *races out.*)

FRYBURGER. Why is he in such a hurry?

TOM. He must be nauseous. Miss Doemaker, while we're waiting, do you mind if we ask you some questions? We really don't know very much about you. Could you tell us a little something about yourself? After all, we just checked up on a nun.

JANE. I'll tell you anything you want to know.

TOM. Okay, let's see...where do you live? What do you do? How did you know about this will reading? Why did you show up? When...

FRYBURGER. Mr. Buckle. You sound suspicious.

TOM. I am suspicious. Do you mind?

JANE. No, I don't mind. I read about the will reading in the paper. I showed up...not for the money – my family has money – I don't need any more... *(Starting to cry.)* I came here today because I loved Mr. Buckle. You're all so wrapped up in how much money you're all getting. I didn't think anyone would mind my being here. Maybe I should leave. If you're so worried about how much money you're getting, you can have whatever I was going to get.

TOM. How much do you think that would be?

JANE. *(Sobbing.)* I'm going to pack and go home.

> (**JANE** *continues sobbing.*)

TOM. I was just asking. Wait. I'm sorry. Don't go. Please. Forgive me, I'm very upset. You have to understand. With grandfather dying and my brother having the mumps and everything. I'm really a nice person. I didn't mean anything by it and I like having you here.

> (**JANE** *stops crying on cue and turns back to* **TOM**, *all smiles.*)

JANE. You mean, you want me to stay?

TOM. Very much.

FRYBURGER. Don't pay any attention to him, Miss Doemaker. It's easy to see how that side of the family became the black sheep. *(To* **TOM**.*)* I can't tell you the difference between the behavior of you and your brother and that of your Cousin Lisa. It's like two completely different families.

TOM. Keep thinking that. *(To* **JANE**.*)* Are you all right?

JANE. Much better. Thank you.

> (**BILLY** *darts in, adjusting his wimple and gasping for air.*)

FRYBURGER. What's wrong with you? You're all out of breath.

BILLY. Well... Billy said to hurry. I hate to keep people waiting.

FRYBURGER. That's exactly what I mean. Billy holds us up, and Sister Fernando hates to keep us waiting.

> (**BILLY** *shoots the others a cocky look.*)

If you'll be seated we can begin. Sister, would you care to sit by me?

BILLY. Who wouldn't? If I wasn't married to the Church, I'd go for you. You're a looker, you know.

FRYBURGER. *(Blushing.)* Oh, Sister.

TOM. Oh, brother.

> (**BILLY** *sits, legs apart.*)

FRYBURGER. Everybody comfortable?

VIRGINIA. Read the damn thing.

FRYBURGER. This will has remained sealed until today. And I'm proud to say that this is the first bit of business I've ever done since passing the Bar.

VIRGINIA. Read the damn thing, Fryburger. Nobody cares where you do your drinking.

FRYBURGER. I just thought I'd mention it.

TOM. I find it very exciting. *(To* **BILLY.***)* I have to talk to you.

FRYBURGER. *(Reading.)* "I, Theodore Buckle, being of sound mind..."

VIRGINIA. Ha!

FRYBURGER. "...hereby bequeath all my earthly possessions in the following manner. To Virginia, my loyal domestic..."

VIRGINIA. He makes me sound like cheap booze.

FRYBURGER. "To Virginia, my loyal domestic, who stood by me all these years... I leave the entire contents..."

> (**TOM** *and* **BILLY** *look worried.* **VIRGINIA** *rises, glowing.*)

"...of my wine cellar."

VIRGINIA. He was a saint that man. A saint.

*(Behind everyone's backs, **VIRGINIA** gives Mr. Buckle an "Italian salute.")*

FRYBURGER. "To my good for nothing grandsons, Tom & Billy..."

TOM. I knew he'd remember us.

FRYBURGER. "...who caused me nothing but heartache, grief and agony their entire lives. I'm sure they believe I haven't left them a nickel. You're wrong boys. Here's a nickel."

*(**FRYBURGER** rips a nickel off of the will and hands it to **TOM**.)*

TOM. I don't believe it. I never liked that man.

BILLY. *(Impressed.)* Buffalo head!

TOM. It's true, I tell you.

FRYBURGER. "To my beautiful adopted granddaughter Lisa."

VIRGINIA. Look again.

FRYBURGER. "I leave the remainder of my estate. All of my wealth."

TOM. Psst. That's you.

BILLY. I always liked that man. You're right, Virginia. He was a saint.

FRYBURGER. "Signed the First of April, 1979, et cetera and so on...and so forth, and et cetera." Well, congratulations, Sister.

BILLY. Thank you. And congratulations to you, Mister Fryburger. You read so well.

JANE. He didn't even mention me. He didn't have to leave me anything but he could have at least said hello.

TOM. A nickel.

JANE. Actually, I'm very glad for you, Sister. Somebody's going to be very happy.

BILLY. You can say that again.

VIRGINIA. What's the date on that will?

FRYBURGER. The First of April, 1979.

VIRGINIA. You don't suppose this is a big April Fool's joke.

FRYBURGER. I'm afraid not. Well, it looks like we're your guests. Tomorrow evening everything will be turned over into your hands.

BILLY. Good, because...tomorrow evening?

TOM. That's too late.

FRYBURGER. Too late for what?

TOM. Sister has to be leaving before tomorrow evening.

BILLY. No, I don't. I don't have to leave until Monday. My Mother Superior called, remember?

TOM. Oh yes. That's right. How about an advance then? I'm sure Sister would like to have a big party to celebrate her inheritance. And of course to congratulate you on your first case since passing the Bar.

FRYBURGER. That would be very nice. I'd be honored. I'm sure we just charge everything. Surely the Buckle credit will not be questioned.

BILLY. No more borrowing, please. As we say in the church, "Never a borrower nor a lender be."

JANE. Didn't Shakespeare say that?

BILLY. He got it from us!

VIRGINIA. I'll go to market and get some goodies.

(**VIRGINIA** *heads for the closet.*)

Let me get my coat.

BILLY. No!

VIRGINIA. Why not?

BILLY. Why not, Tom?

TOM. Because you don't work here anymore, Virginia. There's no reason for you to go shopping ever again.

VIRGINIA. And where am I supposed to go? Forty-seven years I've been in this house. I'm an institution.

BILLY. Of course you are. I wasn't going to let you go, Virginia. After I turn this house over into the "Theodore

Buckle Orphanage," I'll need someone just like you to take care of the place.

VIRGINIA. An orphanage? I'd like that.

BILLY. Of course you would. But today, you relax. No shopping. And no cleaning.

VIRGINIA. I'd like that too. Thank you, Lisa. It's nice that they taught you manners in that place.

BILLY. Now, would you clear the tea things away?

VIRGINIA. Yes ma'am. Yes Sister.

> (**VIRGINIA** *goes to the tea cart and begins wheeling it off.* **TOM** *lifts the dome lid to see whether or not they remembered to remove the baby.*)

TOM. Just checking.

> (**FRYBURGER** *mixes himself a drink at the bar.*)

VIRGINIA. You know, Sister. Sometimes I hear voices too. Do you think He's talking to me? I don't hear them through the television set. But sometimes the garbage disposal says the most obscene things.

> (*She cackles a dirty laugh, remembering.*)

> (**VIRGINIA** *exits with the cart, laughing to herself. The others react.*)

TOM. Well, Lisa, I guess you must be pretty happy. You've been left enough money to live like a queen.

> (*We hear a rapping noise coming from the closet.*)

FRYBURGER. What was that?

> (**FRYBURGER** *looks up, nervous.*)

Mr. Buckle? Is that you?

> (*We hear more noises from the closet.* **FRYBURGER** *turns to it.*)

Did you hear anything?

(BILLY shakes his head "no.")

TOM. I didn't hear anything. Did you Jane?

JANE. I didn't hear anything.

FRYBURGER. I distinctly heard a noise in that closet.

(FRYBURGER heads for the closet. BILLY and TOM cut him off.)

BILLY. There's nothing in that closet.

TOM. It might be a rat.

FRYBURGER. *(Looking around the floor, nervous.)* A rat?

TOM. Yes. Sometimes in these old houses, rats get in the closets.

BILLY. *(Catching on.)* That's true. Any rats in there?

(We hear a squeal of fright from inside the closet.)

FRYBURGER. What the hell was that? There is someone in there.

(He heads for the closet but TOM stops him, thinking faster than ever before.)

TOM. Ah...ha...ha...ha...ah, very good, Sister. Very good. You fooled Mr. Fryburger.

FRYBURGER. Very good? What's very good? What are you talking about?

TOM. Isn't she marvelous? You're throwing your voice again, Sister. *(Laughs.)* God, I love that stuff. I could have sworn I heard a voice coming from the closet, but it was just Sister Fernando...and her ven-tri-lo-quism.

(BILLY catches on.)

JANE. "Ven-tri-lo-quism?"

BILLY. Yes, that's true. As you can see, the closet is completely empty.

(BILLY opens the door a crack and slams it shut so quickly that no one could have seen anything.)

FRYBURGER. Yeah. I need a drink.

>(**FRYBURGER** *mixes himself another scotch.*)

JANE. Boy, I'm impressed. How did you ever learn that stuff, Sister?

BILLY. Paul Winchell spoke at our church once. May I have some water?

FRYBURGER. Certainly.

>(**FRYBURGER** *pours and hands a glass of water to a nervous* **BILLY**.)

Boy, you could have fooled me. I could have sworn I heard a woman screaming in there.

TOM. Yeah, she drives them crazy in the confessionals.

JANE. I think I saw your lips move, Sister. Sorry.

BILLY. Oh, don't be sorry.

>(**BILLY** *drinks nervously.*)

FRYBURGER. Do some more.

BILLY. No, I'm not really very good.

JANE. Oh please?

BILLY. No. Really.

>(**BILLY** *sips his water.*)

GIRL. *(Offstage.)* Help!! Let me out!!

>(**BILLY** *spits his water all over* **TOM**.)

FRYBURGER. Fantastic!

BILLY. Oh, it's not so good.

>(**BILLY** *nervously takes another sip. The baby cries.* **BILLY** *spits his water again.*)

FRYBURGER. A baby crying! This is unbelievable!

BILLY. I'm amazed I'm getting away with it.

JANE. *(Impressed.)* Hey, that is good!

FRYBURGER. Sister, is there anything you can't do?

BILLY. There's a lot I can't do. I'm a nun.

JANE. You must teach me to do that. I really heard a baby crying.

JANE. I have unfinished business down here.

TOM. So do I. First things first.

JANE. Sister, you'd better come up with me where it's safe.

(**JANE** *takes* **BILLY** *by the hand.*)

TOM. Sister, you'll be fine right down here.

JANE. What if you meet up with the prowler?

TOM. Then she can talk him out of his life of crime. Up you go.

(**JANE** *exits.*)

I think she's in love with Fryburger. What a revolting thought.

BILLY. I like her.

TOM. What unfinished business does she have down here?

BILLY. What am I? The Amazing Kreskin or something? How am I supposed to know?

TOM. I thought your girlfriend was going to cooperate. She almost put us behind bars.

BILLY. It's a good thing you thought of rats in the closet. Fryburger would have looked in there for sure.

TOM. I told you I had everything under control.

BILLY. Yeah, like me having leprosy. Jane had to cover for me a couple of times today. I told you I didn't have enough time to prepare for this.

TOM. Do you realize what you just said? She could have given us away but she didn't. She saved us from exposure.

BILLY. Yeah. What coincidences. We've been pretty lucky.

TOM. "Lucky"? Who was it that called you on the phone before?

BILLY. My Mother Superior.

TOM. Billy, there's nobody here now. Who was it, really?

BILLY. The Mother Superior of my convent.

TOM. Something fishy is going on here.

BILLY. Yeah. Who's in the kitchen?

TOM. Nobody. Virginia's hearing things. Any woman who talks to garbage disposals isn't playing with a full deck. Don't you see what I'm getting at? Somebody knows what we're up to.

BILLY. That's what's got me scared. I'm gonna be struck by lightning!

TOM. Not Him. Somebody in this house.

BILLY. Jane? She was in the room when I got my phone call. Besides, if she knows what's going on, why would she keep her mouth shut?

TOM. I don't know.

BILLY. Can we let my girl out of the closet? She's gonna smell of moth balls.

TOM. We'd better hide her upstairs until all of this is over with. At least until we find out what's going on. Open that closet.

BILLY. Hey, if she's not really Lisa, then who is she?

TOM. That's your problem. She's your girlfriend. You put her in there.

BILLY. My problem? This was your idea. Your great plan.

TOM. Didn't she even tell you her name?

BILLY. I never asked.

TOM. Then what were you two doing in there?

BILLY. None of your B-I-business.

TOM. Billy, open up that closet. Now, how are we going to keep her out of the way? Do you think you can keep her busy with something upstairs?

BILLY. Can I keep her busy? You watch me. She's putty in my hands. Hey, are mumps communicable?

TOM. Would you open that closet!!

(**BILLY** *opens the closet door and the* **GIRL** *and her baby hobble out.*)

GIRL. HEEELP!

(**TOM** *cups his hand over her mouth.*)

TOM. What's the matter with you? Are you trying to give us away? Are you trying to get us caught?

(She nods "yes.")

Well, cut it out!

GIRL. What is this place? What's going on here?

BILLY. I'm Billy and that's Tom...

GIRL. Why is he dressed like a nun?

TOM. Well, he's a little crazy. Please hear us out. Everything Billy told you is true. Everything.

GIRL. Everything?

TOM. A man really is coming here to kill us. We don't know who you are. That's not important now. But it is important that you don't give us away. It could mean our lives and yours too. If he thinks you're with us, it could be dangerous for you too.

GIRL. I hadn't thought of that.

BILLY. Well, think about that.

TOM. You must believe us. Billy told you the truth. Every word.

GIRL. You mean, he really is a movie producer?

TOM. What?

GIRL. He told me he was a movie producer.

BILLY. *(Winking.)* I thought it would make things easier.

TOM. Look, he said he was a movie producer but he really isn't.

GIRL. Why is he dressed like a nun?

TOM. He's not really a nun either. He's a little crazy. We all are here today.

GIRL. Omigod. I know where I am now. I knew I had the wrong address. This is that place!

BILLY. What are you talking about?

GIRL. Omigod this is that place!

TOM. What place?

GIRL. Are you both patients here?

BILLY. Patients? What are you talking about?

GIRL. Don't hurt me.

TOM. Why would we want to hurt you?

GIRL. Promise me you won't hurt me?

BILLY. I promise.

GIRL. Why are you two here? What's wrong with you?

BILLY. What makes you think something's wrong with us?

TOM. *(Catching on.)* Well, as you know, sanitariums are crawling with paranoids and the like. Me? I'm merely a petty pickpocket. But I'm cured now.

BILLY. Tom, what are you talking about?

TOM. And Billy, poor boy. Thinks he's a nun.

GIRL. He said he was a movie producer.

TOM. He thinks he's a nun and a movie producer. Schizophrenic. He only wants to produce religious films. He's getting better.

GIRL. You poor thing. Is he harmless?

TOM. As harmless as a fly.

BILLY. Hold it a minute. Can the fly ask a question?

TOM. Yes, Sister DeMille?

BILLY. What the hell are you talking about?

TOM. Quiet, Sister. The warden might hear you.

GIRL. Warden?

TOM. Dear, you'd better hide upstairs. If the warden finds you here, he's bound to think you're a patient too. You'll never get out of here. We're all lifers here. We'll never get out.

GIRL. They make you stay in this place for life? How horrible.

TOM. You'd better hide upstairs.

GIRL. Of course I will. But how will I get out of here?

TOM. We're planning a break-out tonight. Not the really sick people. Just Billy and me. I'm cured, anyway. When the coast is clear, we'll come for you and make a break for it.

LIE, CHEAT, AND GENUFLECT

GIRL. Why don't you just phone for help?

TOM. That's what they want you to do. It's a trap. The phone is hooked up into the warden's office.

GIRL. Oh, that is clever of them. But, what about the man that's coming here to kill you? Who is he?

TOM. He's the man who put us in here. He told everyone we were crazy so he could steal our money and he had us committed here.

GIRL. You mean, you're not really crazy?

TOM. Not us. It's all an act. We've been playing along. Billy's really a Protestant.

GIRL. No kidding? You poor thing. Then all the things you told me in the closet were just an act?

TOM. What did he say in the closet?

(The GIRL whispers in TOM's ear. He grins, then turns and slaps BILLY in the face.)

BILLY. What are you trying to do? Make me stupid? Come on, we can hide up in my room.

GIRL. Is there a place to change a diaper up there?

TOM. *(To BILLY.)* I told you I could handle any situation.

BILLY. How do you think so fast?

(FRYBURGER backs into the room.)

TOM. The warden. Quick. The closet.

(The GIRL ducks into the closet, pulling BILLY in with her.)

Mr. Fryburger!

(FRYBURGER jumps out of his skin.)

FRYBURGER. I can't find anyone. Virginia must be hearing things again.

TOM. You're probably not looking in the right places.

FRYBURGER. I've searched every room, every closet, the entire grounds. There's no where else to look.

TOM. I guess...wait. What's that?

(**FRYBURGER** *freezes and looks up, nervous.*)

FRYBURGER. Mr. Buckle? Mr. Buckle? I don't hear anything.

TOM. That's just it. It's the sound of someone sneaking.

FRYBURGER. I don't hear a thing.

TOM. When you're sneaking around, you never make a sound. That's why it's called sneaking. After them!

FRYBURGER. You go after them. I want a drink.

(**FRYBURGER** *pours himself another scotch.*)

TOM. What happened to your bravery? Jane was very impressed with you. She said she loved man who was brave. I thought you were looking for a prowler.

FRYBURGER. I was looking. I never said I wanted to find him.

TOM. I'll go with you. Follow me.

(**TOM** *and* **FRYBURGER** *sneak offstage. After a beat, we realize* **BILLY** *and the* **GIRL** *are now locked in the closet.* **BILLY** *knocks on the inside of the door.*)

BILLY. (*Offstage.*) Tom!! Psst. Tom!!

(**PIZZA FACE PETRILLO**, *a fiftyish mobster, and his girlfriend,* **MISS MACKINTOSH**, *enter. He dresses stereotype hoodlum and his cheap girlfriend dresses to show off her buxom figure. They sneak around guilty as sin.*)

PIZZA FACE. I told you this is the house. As soon as we find those bums, we'll get out of here.

(**PIZZA FACE** *pulls out a gun to check out the room.*)

MACKINTOSH. Gee, you know everything, Pizza Face.

PIZZA FACE. I told you before. My name is Spencer. Call me that once more and you can forget that singing contract.

MACKINTOSH. Sorry. I'll do whatever you want. You know that, Pizza…

PIZZA FACE. Spencer. You do this one favor for me and I'll do one for you. Remember, if anyone sees us before we find those welching bums...if anyone asks, who we are, I'm a private detective and you're my secretary. "Every private detective's got a Girl Friday."

MACKINTOSH. You're a private dick and I'm your sec-a-tary.

PIZZA FACE. Sec-re-tary.

MACKINTOSH. Sec-a-tary. Ooh. This'll be fun.

*(**MACKINTOSH** blows a big bubble with her gum.)*

PIZZA FACE. Remember, we're arresting them for tax evasion. Then we take the Buckle brothers out to the car.

Then what happens don't concern you.

Come on, they got to be around here somewhere.

*(Gun drawn, **PIZZA FACE** opens the closet door, from behind. We see **SISTER FERNANDO** and the **GIRL** making out. They freeze and stand in fear at the sight of **PIZZA FACE** and **MACKINTOSH**, who do not see them. **PIZZA FACE** and **MACKINTOSH** check over their shoulder for people. From the wine cellar, we hear **VIRGINIA** singing "My Man.")*

MACKINTOSH. I hear a noise.

*(**PIZZA FACE** slams the closet door closed as he and **MACKINTOSH** run for the nearest doorway. **BILLY**'s hand catches the door in time.)*

PIZZA FACE. *(Exiting.)* Quick! In there!

*(**BILLY** exits the closet, his hand throbbing in pain.)*

BILLY. Ow!! Oh, boy, that smarts.

*(We hear **VIRGINIA** singing.)*

GIRL. Who was that man?

BILLY. Ssh. The warden's coming. Hide!

GIRL. Where? I'm not going back in that closet.

BILLY. Oh, yes you are.

GIRL. Let me out of here!

>*(BILLY and the GIRL have a physical tug of war, trying to determine if he can get her into the closet or not. VIRGINIA enters from the wine cellar. She spies BILLY's back end sticking out of the closet. She crosses to him.)*

VIRGINIA. Sister, you're just the one I wanted to see.

>*(BILLY spins around, blockading the door, which remains open. He genuflects to VIRGINIA, who genuflects back. The two bob up and down alternately.)*

I feel terrible and I wanted to talk to someone. Sister, I have a confession.

BILLY. Tell Sister Fernando, child.

VIRGINIA. I'm so ashamed. I've been so greedy. I've been praying and praying for two things all year.

BILLY. And what are they?

VIRGINIA. To be filthy rich. And to have a man for my own play toy.

BILLY. Well, there's your problem. You've got to concentrate on one thing at a time. Now, you go think about what I said and you'll feel much better. And who knows, in His Divine Wisdom, He may feel you deserve something after all.

VIRGINIA. Thank you, Sister. Are you feeling all right? You look flushed.

BILLY. Watch it!

VIRGINIA. Sorry. I didn't mean anything by it.

>*(VIRGINIA exits, genuflecting as she goes.)*

I'll go back to my work now. Thank you, Sister.

>*(VIRGINIA exits into the wine cellar.)*

BILLY. Don't ever do that to a nun!

GIRL. *(Exiting closet.)* Sorry. It's easy to see why she's in here. What a hopeless case. We'd better get upstairs.

BILLY. Do you have everything?

GIRL. Who was that man before?

BILLY. Oh him? Another patient. He thinks he's Al Capone.

GIRL. Who was that girl?

BILLY. Oh her? She's a patient too.

GIRL. She looked like a cheap hooker to me.

BILLY. Nymphomaniac. They're treating her here.

GIRL. Well, you keep away from her.

BILLY. I wouldn't touch her with a ten foot pole.

*(We hear **PIZZA FACE** offstage.)*

Someone's coming. Quick! The closet!

GIRL. I'm sick of the closet. Can't you hide me somewhere else?

BILLY. Every place else is fill up at the moment.

*(**BILLY** pushes her in the closet.)*

GIRL. Let me out of here!

*(As they struggle to go in / get out of the closet, **PIZZA FACE** enters crossing in front of **BILLY** without seeing him. **BILLY** spins around blockading the open closet door again, this time with his hands behind his back.)*

BILLY. Can I help you?

PIZZA FACE. *(Jumping.)* Jesus Christ! You scared the shit out of me...sister.

BILLY. I beg your pardon?

PIZZA FACE. I mean, pardon me Sister, you startled me. I thought I, was alone.

BILLY. *(Looking up.)* We're never alone, my son.

PIZZA FACE. *(Looking up.)* Yeah well. I'm looking for some bums...er...gentlemen named Tom and Billy Buckle. I'm a private dick and I have to run them in.

BILLY. For what?

PIZZA FACE. Tax evasion. That sort of thing. Have you seen them? One's a good-looking guy about twenty-five. And the other one's kind of skinny and homely.

BILLY. He's not homely!

PIZZA FACE. Oh, have you seen them?

BILLY. I've never heard of them. I don't believe we've met. I'm Sister Fernando.

> (**BILLY** *does a quick curtsy.*)

PIZZA FACE. How do you do.

> (**PIZZA FACE** *sticks his hand out to shake hands.* **BILLY** *can't move. Suddenly, the* **GIRL**'s *hand comes out through* **BILLY**'s *arm and shakes hands.*)

BILLY. Oh! Nice to meet you.

> (*The* **GIRL**'s *other hand comes out on* **BILLY**'s *left. From here until the end of the scene they act as* **BILLY**'s *hands would, although they are quite feminine.*)

PIZZA FACE. My, but your hands are soft.

BILLY. You try washing dishes in a convent.

PIZZA FACE. The name's Petrillo. Spencer Petrillo

> (*Business of stroking* **BILLY**'s *chin and snapping fingers to remember.*)

BILLY. Petrillo? Where have I heard that name before? Let me see...

PIZZA FACE. It's a common name.

BILLY. Oh well. I'm sorry to disappoint you, but those two gentlemen aren't here at all.

PIZZA FACE. Ain't this that place where they're reading that will?

BILLY. Yes, but that's all over with. They've gone home now.

> (*The* **GIRL**'s *thumb points the way.*)

PIZZA FACE. I thought you never heard of them.

BILLY. There were so many people here today. I have trouble remembering names.

(Business of stroking head.)

I have trouble remembering my own name lately. Plus I have all those saints to keep track of.

(The hands begin counting saints.)

PIZZA FACE. Well, if you don't mind, I'm gonna look around some more.

*(Hands to **BILLY**'s chest.)*

BILLY. Mind?

(Hands wave away from chest.)

Why would we mind? We have nothing to hide here.

PIZZA FACE. Thanks Sis.

*(As **PIZZA FACE** turns to leave, **MISS MACKINTOSH** enters from the opposite side.)*

MACKINTOSH. Hey, Pizza Face!

BILLY. Pizza Face?

*(The **GIRL**'s hands go to the sides of **BILLY**'s face in shock.)*

PIZZA FACE. Ah, here's my secretary, Miss MacKintosh.

BILLY. I won't have any trouble, remembering that name. I'll just think of the apples.

*(The **GIRL** slaps **BILLY**'s face.)*

MACKINTOSH. Yes, I'm Mr. Petrillo's sec-a-tary. Every private detective's got a Girl Friday.

BILLY. Then you must be very successful, Mr. Petrillo. Today's only Wednesday.

PIZZA FACE. They've given us free run of the house, Miss MacKintosh.

BILLY. Yes, you might want to locate a Mr. Fryburger. He's in charge here.

PIZZA FACE. You're most kind, Sister.

BILLY. That's my job.

> (**BILLY** *blows on the* **GIRL**'s *fingertips and she rubs them across his chest in mock-modesty.*)

PIZZA FACE. Oh, if you see any of those Buckle Brothers, don't tell them I'm looking for them. I'd like to... surprise them.

> (**PIZZA FACE** *pats his gun.*)

BILLY. We'll keep it just between you and me and of course Him.

> (*The* **GIRL** *points up.*)

PIZZA FACE. Shall we, Miss MacKintosh?

MACKINTOSH. Sure, I'd love to. Where you wanna go?

PIZZA FACE. Why, to find Mr. Fryburger.

MACKINTOSH. Nice meeting you, Sister.

> (**MACKINTOSH** *and the* **GIRL**'s *hand shake hands.*)

BILLY. I really think you're wasting your time. The boys left hours ago.

> (*The* **GIRL** *points to watch.*)

PIZZA FACE. That's impossible, Sister. I followed them here.

BILLY. Then, you'd recognize them if you saw them?

> (**GIRL** *shades* **BILLY**'s *face with her hand.*)

PIZZA FACE. Of course. I just described them to you, didn't I?

MACKINTOSH. I think they're cute. Especially the little homely one.

BILLY. He's not homely.

> (**GIRL** *pinches* **BILLY**'s *cheek.*)

PIZZA FACE. Well, we'd better be on our way.

BILLY. Have a safe trip.

> (**GIRL** *waves goodbye.*)

May Saint Bernard be with you.

(GIRL crosses herself – BILLY.)

PIZZA FACE. Thank you.

(PIZZA FACE and MACKINTOSH exit. BILLY slams the closet door closed and dashes off in the opposite direction.)

BILLY. Tom! Tom!

GIRL. *(Inside closet.)* Let me out! Billy!

(JANE enters from upstairs. She hears the GIRL's screams.)

JANE. This has waited long enough.

(JANE opens the closet and addresses the GIRL. She never sees the baby inside.)

All right, you. Get out here. I'd like to have a word with you.

GIRL. There's been a mistake. I'm not supposed to be in here.

JANE. Then step out. Who the hell do you think you are? You're not Lisa.

GIRL. Everybody keeps calling me Lisa. They all think I'm Lisa Buckle.

JANE. You aren't Lisa Buckle. Thought you could get away with it, didn't you? Admit it.

GIRL. No. But every time I try to leave they lock me in that closet. *(Gasps.)* Uh oh.

(The GIRL points to JANE.)

Patient?

JANE. Normally.

GIRL. Oh. Then you work here?

JANE. I used to work here. Now, I'm a visitor just like you.

GIRL. Just like me? Do they make you stay in the closet too?

JANE. What have those two done to you?

GIRL. Nothing. I'm fine. And they haven't harmed my baby either.

(**JANE** *studies the* **GIRL**'s *pregnantless shape.*)

JANE. Baby? And they've been throwing you into closets? I didn't think they'd go that far.

GIRL. Everything's all right. Tom gave me my baby.

JANE. Tom? Tom gave you a baby? You mean...you and he are romantically involved?

GIRL. Oh no. Billy's the one I like. I didn't want to go along with any of this, but Billy talked me into it.

JANE. If you're in love with Billy, why did Tom give you a baby?

GIRL. At the time, Billy couldn't.

JANE. What a generous brother.

GIRL. He didn't mind.

JANE. Didn't you mind?

GIRL. Of course not. What a cute little thing.

JANE. I wouldn't know.

GIRL. You'd love him, really. It wasn't so bad. But frankly I was a little scared. I don't really know Billy and Tom all that well.

JANE. It wasn't so bad? I thought he was a real ladies man. Listen, I had no idea about Tom and your baby...this gets better by the minute. You can go wait in your closet and do whatever it is you do in there.

GIRL. You won't turn me in to the warden, will you?

JANE. I won't say a word.

GIRL. I want to get out of here.

JANE. Sure you do. Especially in your condition.

GIRL. You won't turn me in to the warden, will you?

JANE. Who do you mean, Fryburger?

GIRL. I guess so.

JANE. Look, it sounds ridiculous, but I have to give him credit. He doesn't give up. I want to see how this turns out. You continue your charade. I'll keep my mouth shut.

GIRL. Thank you. You're very kind.

JANE. How long are you supposed to stay in the closet?

GIRL. Actually, I'm supposed to stay upstairs until they come to get me so we can make our escape. I don't want to be a lifer.

JANE. They never stop. Do they?

GIRL. I don't think so.

JANE. You'd better get up there, then. Listen, I'll cover for you if you'll cover for me. If anyone asks who I am, I'm Jane the Nurse.

GIRL. Jane the Nurse. Will my baby and I be safe up there?

JANE. As long as Fryburger doesn't try mauling you too.

(**JANE** *exits, the* **GIRL** *reaches back inside the open closet and retrieves her baby and bag.*)

GIRL. You poor little thing. This has been quite a day for you. Come on, little Russell, let's go upstairs where it's safe.

(*The* **GIRL** *and the baby exit upstairs.*)

MACKINTOSH. (*Entering from the opposite side.*) Mr. Spencer? Psst. Pizza Face!

(*She whistles a piercing whistle.*)

This ain't no fun no more! I thought I'd just have to sleep with him, I didn't think I'd have to be any sec-a-tary. Pizza Face? I don't want to get caught here.

(*She edges her way to the closet.*)

I'll wait in here.

(*As* **MACKINTOSH** *closes the closet,* **BILLY** *enters dressed back in his "street clothes."*)

BILLY. Tom? Where are you?

(*He notices the closet.*)

Oh! Let me get you out of there. I'll never keep you in a closet again. I've been in love with you from the second I saw you today. Let me get you out of there. We can go upstairs. It'll be very romantic, just you and me and me and you. What do you say?

(**BILLY** *opens the closet and out steps* **MISS MACKINTOSH**. *She sizes him up quickly.*)

MACKINTOSH. Sure!

(**MACKINTOSH** *drags* **BILLY** *by the hand out the door.* **BILLY**, *confused, glances back at the closet.*)

TOM. (*Entering from the opposite side.*) Billy? Where is everybody? I'm starting to hear voices.

(**TOM** *goes to the closet.*)

Come on, you two, get out of there.

(*He opens the closet. It is empty.*)

How'd they get out of there?

(**JANE** *squeals offstage.* **TOM** *starts to hide himself in the closet but changes his mind.*)

Oh, no you don't.

(**TOM** *dashes off the same direction* **PIZZA FACE** *exited, as* **JANE** *enters, being chased by a soused* **FRYBURGER**.)

JANE. Look, Mr. Fryburger...

FRYBURGER. Bob. Call me Bob. You tigress. You tigress.

JANE. Mr. Fryburger! Look, we can't be seen together. What would people think?

FRYBURGER. They'd think I did all right.

JANE. I have a reputation. Please. We really must be discreet.

FRYBURGER. I suppose you're right. This is my first case. I'd hate to have word get back to my office.

JANE. Of course you would. Why don't you wait in the closet and we can rendezvous later.

FRYBURGER. Why the closet?

JANE. Who would ever think of looking in there?

FRYBURGER. I wouldn't.

(*He backs himself into the closet.*)

Don't be long, my dear.

(**TOM** *enters and* **JANE** *slams the door shut in* **FRYBURGER**'s *face.*)

TOM. Hide me. Hide me.

(**TOM** *heads for the closet and* **JANE** *stops him.*)

JANE. Don't go in there!

TOM. Why? Have you looked in there already?

JANE. Don't tell me you're hiding something in that closet?

TOM. No. What makes you think that? I'm hiding nothing in that closet.

(**TOM** *opens the closet to prove his point. We see* **FRYBURGER** *with his pants halfway off.* **TOM** *shuts the door and reacts to what he's seen.* **TOM** *reopens the closet as* **FRYBURGER** *tries to dress and look casual.*)

Mr. Fryburger, what are you doing in that closet?

FRYBURGER. Uh...checking for rats. Sometimes in these old houses, rats get into the closet. Nope. No rats here.

JANE. We might as well let the cat out of the bag, Mr. Fryburger. Bob.

TOM. Bob?

JANE. You see, Tom, Bob and I are in love.

(**FRYBURGER** *drops his briefcase.*)

FRYBURGER. "In love"?

TOM. I knew it. I knew you'd go for the Fryburger type.

FRYBURGER. What do you mean by that?

JANE. Don't get upset, dear. Here.

(**JANE** *holds out a skeleton key.*)

Here's the key to my room. You go on up. I won't be but a moment. The bed's already turned down.

FRYBURGER. The bed?

(**FRYBURGER** *takes the key in a daze.*)

JANE. Yes, the soft thing with four legs and pillows. Hurry, my dearest.

FRYBURGER. But I didn't bring any pajamas.

JANE. Let's not delay a moment longer, Bob. You tiger.

> (**JANE** *roars at him and he roars like a tiger back.* **FRYBURGER** *quickly exits up the stairs.*)

TOM. That's disgusting. What a disgusting display of public affection. I knew you'd go for the Fryburger type. He's rich. He's got money...

JANE. Don't tell me you're jealous?

TOM. Of him? Why should I be?

JANE. For one thing, he's a gentleman. And for another thing, he doesn't use innocent people to get ahead.

TOM. What do you know? I mean...what do you mean? Why did you say that?

JANE. I know all about the girl in the closet and the baby you gave her. I know all about Sister Fernando. I know all about Pizza Face Petrillo. I know all about your debt.

TOM. How about the Mother Superior? You know anything about the Mother Superior?

JANE. How would I know that? I was in the room when she called. Incidentally, this is the most ridiculous scheme anyone's ever tried to get away with. You know nothing about nuns, nothing about diseases, nothing about inheritances...

TOM. For your information, we did get away with it. That is, until about two minutes ago.

JANE. What do you mean?

TOM. Pizza Face Petrillo followed us here. He's in the house. I just saw him.

JANE. Why would he show up here himself. If he wanted you, he'd just send some of his boys.

TOM. He doesn't have any boys. He doesn't even drive a Cadillac. He's got a '69 Catalina. He's come here to get us.

JANE. I'm sure you can lie your way out of this one too.

TOM. You think I'm proud of what I've done here? I blew my brothers life savings away at the tracks on bets he didn't even know about. I took an innocent girl and took advantage of her. That's the part I feel worst about.

JANE. Well, at least you feel some remorse.

TOM. Hey, I tried to make her as comfortable as possible. I gave her sandwiches and Dr. Pepper before we even started.

JANE. Real romantic.

TOM. Please help me.

JANE. I won't let him find you.

> (**BILLY** *dashes in, disheveled and blowing a bubble.*)

BILLY. Hide me. Hide yourself. We've got company.

> (**BILLY** *chews gum as* **TOM** *and* **JANE** *react.*)

Oh, hello my child.

> (**BILLY** *genuflects.*)

JANE. Cut the crap, Sister.

> (**BILLY** *feels for his wimple, realizing he is out of costume.*)

BILLY. She knows?

TOM. Yes, she knows. Where's your robe, jackass?

BILLY. I can't keep this up much longer.

TOM. You may not have to. We'll be laying on the bottom of a river.

BILLY. Why would we want to do that? Have you seen Lisa? She's disappeared.

JANE. Look, Billy, that innocent little girl you both took advantage of is in as much trouble as you two are. She has no idea what's going on.

TOM. That's true. You've confused her good.

BILLY. Me? How is it that you think up everything and I get blamed for everything?

TOM. That's what partners are for.

BILLY. I didn't want to do any of this in the first place. I wish I was dead. What would my father say if he saw me like this? I want to go home.

TOM. You'd better find Lisa and hide with her upstairs. Hide up there until tonight. Then, when everyone's asleep, we can sneak down here and rob the safe. We can't wait until tomorrow.

BILLY. I'm not gonna rob a safe. What I've agreed to do so far is one thing, but I am not going to rob any safe. I've never done anything illegal in my life.

TOM. You've already kidnapped a girl and a baby. You've assaulted the girl. You broke and entered this house. You can be arrested for fraud, grand larceny, shall I go on?

BILLY. What time should we meet down here?

TOM. Midnight.

JANE. May I join you?

TOM. You'd really help us after all of this?

JANE. I don't want to see you killed.

TOM. *(Kisses her.)* You're a doll. Thanks.

(**TOM** *and* **JANE** *go to exit.* **BILLY** *stops them.*)

BILLY. What should I wear? It's bad enough I'm gonna rob a safe. I don't want to have to do it dressed as a nun.

TOM. I don't care what you wear. Just dress dark. Do whatever you have to do to blend into the night!

(**TOM** *and* **JANE** *start to exit again.* **BILLY** *stops them.*)

JANE. What do we do until midnight? I have Fryburger in my bed, waiting for me.

TOM. I'm sure you can pry yourself away by midnight.

BILLY. And what about dinner? I'm a growing boy. I have to eat.

TOM. As long as Pizza Face is in this house, we can't show our faces. Remember. Midnight. Down here. The safe is in here somewhere. Where's my map?

> (**TOM** *and* **JANE** *exit one way,* **BILLY** *the other.* **PIZZA FACE** *enters, pinning* **BILLY** *against the wall.* **MISS MACKINTOSH** *follows in.*)

MACKINTOSH. But I didn't do nothing with him. He ran away.

PIZZA FACE. I knew they were in here. Those monsters forced that saintly nun to lie for them. Wait'll I get my hands on them. I'll tear them limb from limb. Limb from limb. I'll tear them limb from limb!

MACKINTOSH. What do we do now?

PIZZA FACE. You go wait in the car. I'll settle this quickly...

> (**PIZZA FACE** *draws his gun menacingly.*)

PIZZA FACE. ...and quietly.

MACKINTOSH. I'm hungry, Pizza Face. I want some sushi.

PIZZA FACE. What's the matter with you? Can't you see I'm working here?

MACKINTOSH. I was just saying...

> (**PIZZA FACE** *holds out his car keys.*)

PIZZA FACE. Here. Take the car. Go eat, you bottomless pit you. I'll expect you back here in one hour.

MACKINTOSH. *(Blowing a kiss as she exits.)* Bye doll.

PIZZA FACE. *(Calling.)* And put air in the tires!

> (**PIZZA FACE** *sizes up the room and heads for the closet.*)

I'll just duck in here. They're bound to come by here.

> (**PIZZA FACE** *ducks into the closet.* **BILLY** *closes the door and pries himself off the wall. He dashes out to get* **TOM**.)

BILLY. *(Exiting.)* Tom! Tom!

> (**TOM** *enters from the opposite side, with* **JANE** *close behind.*)

TOM. What? ...I'm hearing voices again.

JANE. *(Glancing over her shoulder.)* Are you sure?

TOM. Yes, I'm sure. I just saw the car pull away. The coast is clear. Thank God. Jane, how long have you known about our plan?

JANE. From the beginning. I was standing over there.

TOM. Why didn't you say anything? Why'd you let us get away with everything? I...of course! You can blackmail us! How could I have been so blind? That's why you kept quiet.

JANE. You amaze me.

TOM. 70/30.

JANE. Let's find the safe.

TOM. All right. 60/40. You can split Billy's half.

JANE. Are you sure the safe is in here?

TOM. All right. All right. 50/50. But that's it!

JANE. Where is the safe on the map?

TOM. And you look so innocent.

>   (**TOM** *checks his map.*)

It should be right behind there.

>   (**TOM** *points blindly. Right at the closet.*)

JANE. In the closet?

TOM. Of course! Who would think to look in a closet for a safe? Grandfather was a genius. And now I can get what's coming to me. And to you, too.

>   (**TOM** *opens the closet. We see* **PIZZA FACE**, *gun drawn.* **TOM** *and* **JANE** *shriek with fright and slam the closet door in his face.*)

JANE. Is that?

TOM. It is. Give me a lamp or something.

JANE. Why? I saw him fine.

TOM. Give me a vase. Give me a bottle...

JANE. Oh. You're going to...

(**JANE** *mimes knocking him out.*)

TOM. Would you please hurry.

(**JANE** *grabs an empty liquor bottle off of the bar. She holds it over her head as she approaches the closet, behind* **TOM**'s *shoulder.*)

When I say "Go," I'll open the closet and you let him have it. One... Two... Three... Four... Five. Ready?

JANE. Ready.

(**JANE** *closes her eyes, tense.* **BILLY** *wanders in, behind them. He is curious as to what they're up to and peers over* **JANE**'s *shoulder to better see.*)

TOM. Hey! Pizza Face! I've got something for you! Go!

(**TOM** *swings the closet door open as* **JANE** *swings back with all her might. The bottle shatters on* **BILLY**'s *head. It knocks him cold.* **PIZZA FACE**, **JANE**, *and* **TOM** *all follow* **BILLY**'s *collapse.* **TOM** *and* **JANE** *slowly turn to* **PIZZA FACE**, *who grins real big.*)

PIZZA FACE. *(Chuckling.)* Yeah? What was it that you had for me?

(**TOM** *indicates the shattered remains of the bottle.*)

TOM. Oh, just a little something.

PIZZA FACE. And now, I've got something for you. Welcher.

(**JANE** *pitches a vase at* **PIZZA FACE**, *which knocks him cold.*)

TOM. Good shot. Where'd you learn that?

JANE. I used to pitch for a girl's softball team.

TOM. You saved my life!

(**TOM** *grabs her and kisses her.* **JANE** *pulls him into a romantic kiss. Finally, it breaks.*)

JANE. Wow. *(Lovestruck.)* We've got to get them out of here before someone named Fryburger comes in here. If he sees this, you'll lose all of that money for sure.

TOM. Yeah. And you too. We can hide them upstairs. After midnight when we rob the safe, we can pay him off and get him out of here. You take him and I'll take him.

> (**TOM** *lifts* **BILLY** *up, but* **JANE** *can't even drag* **PIZZA FACE** *an inch.*)

JANE. Could you give me a hand here?

> (**TOM** *drops* **BILLY** *on his face. They switch people with the same results.*)

Wouldn't it be easier one at a time?

> (**TOM** *drops* **PIZZA FACE**, *and they both pick up* **BILLY**. *They begin to climb the staircase.*)

TOM. Right. We can revive Billy upstairs.

JANE. How long has he been masquerading around as a nun?

TOM. Since 3:00. Why?

JANE. I think a nun with five o'clock shadow might look suspicious.

TOM. Right. I've got a razor in my suitcase. I'll shave him myself. I don't know what I'd do without you.

JANE. Keep that thought.

> (*They exit.* **TOM** *calls back down.*)

TOM. *(Exiting.)* Don't go anywhere!

> (**VIRGINIA** *enters from the wine cellar. She is drunk worse than we've seen her. She staggers through the room singing "My Man." She passes* **PIZZA FACE**. *She does a double-take. In his new position, he looks like a gift under a Christmas tree.*)

VIRGINIA. A man!

> (*She looks up to heaven.*)

Thank you, God!

> (**VIRGINIA** *drags* **PIZZA FACE** *into the cellar, muttering to herself.*)

Thank you, thank you, thank you. Look at that hair! Come on baby! Put your arm around me. Attaboy. I know what you need. What a bod. Come to mama. I'll take you downstairs to my little spot. I've got what you need baby. Thank you, God.

> (**VIRGINIA** *looks up to God for one last thank you.*)

My prayers have been answered!

> (*They disappear into the wine cellar as* **TOM** *and* **JANE** *dash into the room.*)

TOM. You take his arms and I'll take his legs.

> (*They dash to where the body was and as they go to pick it up, realize that he's no longer there.*)

JANE. Somebody already took them.

TOM. Mr. Petrillo? Yoo-hoo. Anybody home?

> (**TOM** *cautiously opens the closet door. It is empty.*)

JANE. He's gone!

> (**TOM** *and* **JANE** *look to each other in fear.*)
>
> (*Curtain.*)

End of Act Two

ACT III

(At Rise: The stage is dark. It is midnight. We see someone sneaking down the stairs, carrying a briefcase. He wears pajamas. He flips the light switch on and we see it is **FRYBURGER**. *He checks his watch and continues his search.)*

FRYBURGER. Jane? Where are you, you tigress? You tease. I love hiding games. Jane? I'll find you, you tigress. You've got to be around here somewhere. Yoo-hoo! Woo-hoo!

(He exits offstage on his hunt. From the stop of the stairs, **TOM**, **JANE**, *and* **BILLY** *dash in. They are all dressed in black.* **TOM** *and* **JANE** *wear football black tape under each eye.* **BILLY** *wears his as eyebrows and a mustache looking like Groucho Marx. They creep down the stairs in unison.)*

TOM. Remember, we can't get caught. We can't be seen.

*(***BILLY*** points at the lights, which are on.)*

BILLY. But Tom...

TOM. Ssh. We've got to remain invisible.

BILLY. But Tom...

TOM. Ssh. Would you remain quiet before you give us away?

JANE. Tom?

TOM. What?

JANE. The lights are on.

TOM. Oh. Billy, hit the switch.

BILLY. What?

TOM. Turn the lights off. That was burglar talk.

(**BILLY** *turns the lights off.*)

BILLY. I'm starving to death. That was hunger talk.

JANE. Me too. Mr. Fryburger had to eat all by himself. I'll bet he got suspicious.

TOM. I'll bet he's still waiting for you in the bed.

JANE. Where do you suppose Pizza Face is waiting? We've searched this whole house.

TOM. My guess is that he left. He must have realized who he's dealing with.

BILLY. If he's gone, why are we bothering to rob the safe to pay him back?

TOM. I'm no welcher. We owe him money. We're going to pay him the money.

BILLY. You amaze me. We're robbing a safe to keep your name clean with a loan shark? You've got a warped sense of priorities.

TOM. Look, you want him to come back here with ten thugs?

BILLY. You said he didn't have any thugs.

TOM. He could rent.

JANE. Would you two stop. Let's get this over with. Who's got the map?

BILLY. Why do we need a map? You said the safe was right in the closet.

TOM. Well, it's dark in here. We have to be sure of where it is.

(**BILLY** *flips on the lights.*)

BILLY. *(Pointing.)* It's right over there...

TOM & JANE. Turn the lights off!

(**BILLY** *flips the lights off.*)

TOM. I hope for your sake that Fryburger didn't see that.

JANE. I thought he was waiting for me in my bed upstairs.

TOM. He's been there for six hours. Nothing's worth that long a wait.

JANE. Well, you'll never know, will you?

FRYBURGER. *(Offstage.)* Where are you, tigress?

> *(**FRYBURGER** roars, as **TOM** and **BILLY** hide in the darkness of the room.)*

(Entering.) Ah, there you are.

JANE. Mr. Fryburger!

FRYBURGER. Have you been hiding from me? I'll have to discipline you.

> *(**FRYBURGER** begins stalking **JANE** around the room.)*

JANE. Mr. Fryburger...

> *(**FRYBURGER** roars.)*

BILLY. What's he doing?

TOM. Ssh.

> *(We hear a slap.)*

BILLY. Don't ever hit me there. You know about my problem.

FRYBURGER. *(Freezing.)* Is someone there? Mr. Buckle?

JANE. No, it's just me, Mr. Fryburger. I've been waiting for you.

FRYBURGER. Where's the light switch?

JANE. Oh, leave them off. It's better that way.

FRYBURGER. Anything you say, darling. How about a big fat kiss?

JANE. Why?

FRYBURGER. I've been waiting for six hours.

> *(**FRYBURGER** grabs her in a clinch. **JANE** calls to **TOM**.)*

JANE. Uh... Do something!

FRYBURGER. Very well.

> *(**FRYBURGER** tries to kiss **JANE** in the dark. **TOM** and **BILLY** make stomping noises as if they've just entered the room.)*

TOM. Well, here we are.

BILLY. Yup. Here we are.

> (**FRYBURGER** *pulls away and strains to see them in the dark.*)

FRYBURGER. What do you two want? Can't you see we want to be alone?

TOM. No, I can't.

BILLY. How can we see anything? The lights are off.

TOM. That's why we're looking for you, Mr. Fryburger. It seems that the lights have gone off.

BILLY. Of course they're off. I turned them off.

TOM. I know you did, Billy. But we must have blown a fuse.

FRYBURGER. Well, I like the dark.

TOM. Mr. Fryburger, you're the only one who can fix it. We don't know where the fuse box is.

FRYBURGER. Can't it wait until morning? You two should be in bed anyway.

BILLY. I sleep with a nightlight.

JANE. Oh, you'd better fix them, Mr. Fryburger. It's better with the lights on.

FRYBURGER. I thought it was better in the dark.

JANE. I like them to go on and off. That's the best.

FRYBURGER. Oh. Well, I'll go fix them. Anything for you, my dear. Are you positive they're off?

TOM. You can see for yourself.

FRYBURGER. I suppose so. I won't be but a moment, tigress.

JANE. I'll wait for you. Upstairs.

FRYBURGER. No hiding this time. Wait for me right here.

> (**FRYBURGER** *roars at* **JANE** *and exits with his briefcase, out the archway.*)

BILLY. There's nothing wrong with the lights. See?

> (**BILLY** *flips the lights on.* **TOM** *dives at the switch, but it is too late.*)

TOM. I hope he didn't see that. It's too late now. Billy, get upstairs and get dressed as Sister Fernando.

BILLY. Why? I want to rob the safe too.

TOM. We're running out of time. You get dressed. We'll rob the safe while he's down fixing the lights. Then we can get the hell out of here and Sister Fernando can make the drop for us and pay back Pizza Face. We can do this in about ten minutes. Let's get moving.

BILLY. Why do I have to pay him back as Sister Fernando? It's bad enough I have to do that indoors. I'm not going out on the street dressed like that.

TOM. Just get dressed.

BILLY. What if Fryburger comes back up here? He'll see you.

TOM. I can explain my way out of anything.

BILLY. How are you going to explain that black junk all over your face?

TOM. Why'd we wear this stuff? You go dress and we'll go wash.

> (**BILLY** *heads the way as he,* **TOM** *and* **JANE** *race up the stairs. As they exit, the wine cellar door opens and* **PIZZA FACE** *enters. He is dressed in boxer shorts, a silk tank undershirt, socks with garters, shoes and his hat. He is very confused. We see lipstick marks. He rubs his head.)*

PIZZA FACE. I'm getting out of here.

> (**PIZZA FACE** *glances down at himself.)*

What the hell am I wearing? What's going on here? Oh, my head!

> (**VIRGINIA** *enters from the cellar in a hot pink negligee. Her make-up is as thick as ever. She bats her big eyelashes at* **PIZZA FACE**.)

VIRGINIA. Where are you going, lover boy?

PIZZA FACE. *(Seeing her for the first time.)* Aah!

> (**PIZZA FACE** *pinches himself.)*

Omigod! I'm awake!

> (**VIRGINIA** *chases* **PIZZA FACE** *around the room.*)

VIRGINIA. Thought you were dreaming, didn't you, lover boy?

PIZZA FACE. Dreaming? I thought I'd gone to hell and died. Where's MacKintosh?

VIRGINIA. Want to go another round?

PIZZA FACE. Get away from me! Where are my pants?

> (**PIZZA FACE** *runs back down into the wine cellar.*)

VIRGINIA. *(Following him into the cellar.)* You'll never need them again!

> (*The* **GIRL** *and her baby creep in from stage left.*)

GIRL. Billy? Where are you? They've gone! They've escaped! They escaped and left me here to be a lifer. I don't want to be a lifer!

FRYBURGER. *(Offstage.)* Jane?

GIRL. The warden!

> (*The* **GIRL** *ducks into the closet. She leaves the door ajar.* **FRYBURGER** *returns to the room, feeling smug.*)

FRYBURGER. Well, I think I know what's wrong with them. It's a faulty fuse, so I'll just…there's nothing wrong with these lights. Tom. Jane. Billy! Where is everybody? What the hell is going on around here?

> (*At the top of the stairs, we see* **TOM** *and* **JANE** *– clean-faced – as they sneak down the stairs, holding hands.* **FRYBURGER** *poses in the archway.*)

TOM. Remember, Fryburger can't see us.

> (**TOM** *tip-toes farther. Directly into* **FRYBURGER**.)

(To **JANE**.*)* I think he sees us.

JANE. Oh, hello.

FRYBURGER. What the hell is going on around here?!

> (**TOM** and **JANE** *jump.*)

Is something going on between you two?

> (**TOM** and **JANE** *drop their hands.*)

TOM. Certainly not.

JANE. Not on a bet.

FRYBURGER. You must take me for a fool.

TOM. I'll remember to do that.

FRYBURGER. I just saw you two holding hands.

> (**TOM** and **JANE** *hide their hands behind their backs.*)

I just spent six hours in an empty bed.

TOM. I hope you brought a book.

FRYBURGER. I had my legal briefs. Yes.

TOM. You seem more like a boxer short man to me.

FRYBURGER. I demand an explanation. All day long, you've done nothing except make me look like a fool. I was sent to the train station to pick up a nun who wasn't there. I ate dinner all alone. I spent six hours in an empty bed. Alone. I just fixed lights that weren't even broken. I'd like to know why.

TOM. We thought the lights were broken. We must have been hitting the wrong switch.

> (**TOM** *plays with the light switch.*)

FRYBURGER. Jane, I'm disappointed. I thought you were sweet on me.

JANE. How I am on you is none of your business.

TOM. Mr. Fryburger, there's a simple explanation for everything.

FRYBURGER. *(Sitting.)* I'd love to hear it. Why did I eat dinner alone?

TOM. Well, sir, Billy, of course, is an easy one to explain. His measles got worse.

JANE. Mumps.

TOM. Mumps, yes. Forgive me. I was speaking rashly.

> *(Behind their backs, The **GIRL** and her baby sneak out of the closet. She tries to escape to the archway, silently. **JANE** sees her and makes nervous sounds.)*

Anyway, he spent the whole day in bed. He couldn't have kept anything down. Right Jane?

JANE. Aah.

TOM. Right. And he kept making noises.

JANE. Aah.

TOM. Weird noises like "aah."

> *(**FRYBURGER** turns to see where **JANE** is looking. The **GIRL** sees **FRYBURGER** and freezes. She lets out a scream which in turn scares **TOM**, who screams. **JANE** screams. **FRYBURGER** screams.)*

FRYBURGER. Hold it right there, young lady. Who is this?

GIRL. I'm not supposed to be in here. I don't want to be a lifer.

FRYBURGER. Mr. Buckle, who is this woman?

TOM. You mean her?

GIRL. *(Clinging to **TOM**.)* Tom, don't let them hurt me.

FRYBURGER. I should have known. Mr. Buckle, have you been sneaking women into this house?

TOM. Yes. This is...my girlfriend.

GIRL. I'm Lisa Buckle.

FRYBURGER. You're who?

GIRL. Lisa Buckle.

TOM. That's right. She's...no! She's...

FRYBURGER. What are you trying to pull? How can she be Lisa Buckle if Sister Fernando is Lisa Buckle?

TOM. Well, that's not so easy to explain... It seems that...

JANE. She really does have a baby! I thought she was just pregnant.

GIRL. Don't hurt my baby!

FRYBURGER. *(To* **JANE.***)* You know her too?

JANE. No. We've never met.

TOM. She says she's Lisa Buckle, but she really isn't. Tell him who you really are.

GIRL. I'm Lisa Buckle.

TOM. See? No!

FRYBURGER. Mr. Buckle, I demand an explanation. Where is Sister Fernando? There certainly can't be two Lisa Buckles.

> (**BILLY**, *as* **SISTER FERNANDO**, *enters the staircase landing. He has forgotten to remove the black tape from his eyebrows and under his nose.)*

JANE. Aah.

FRYBURGER. Where is Sister Fernando?

BILLY. I'm right here, my son.

> (**FRYBURGER** *sees through everything.* **BILLY** *still unaware, genuflects.)*

FRYBURGER. What is on your face?

TOM. Oh…that? In addition to being a great ventriloquist, Sister Fernando does one hell of a Groucho Marx impression. Isn't that right, Sister Fernando?

BILLY. That's the most ridiculous thing I ever heard.

GIRL. What IS that all over your face, Billy?

> (**TOM** *covers her mouth with his hand.)*

FRYBURGER. "Billy"?

TOM. "Silly." She called her "silly." Look at her face with all that grease on it. Sister, you really do look silly.

> (**TOM** *forces a laugh.)*

BILLY. Yes, my son. I do look silly.

> (**BILLY** *and* **TOM** *force laughs.)*

FRYBURGER. Not as silly as you will both look in jail. Before I call the police, would you care to tell me what's going on here today? It's all over, Mr. Buckle.

(**TOM** *smacks* **BILLY**.)

TOM. It's all your fault. Why couldn't you wash your face?

BILLY. My fault? Who let Lisa out of the closet?

GIRL. I'm Lisa Buckle.

FRYBURGER. You're Lisa Buckle. She's Lisa Buckle. (*To* **JANE**.) And I suppose you're Lisa Buckle too.

JANE. As a matter of fact, I am.

FRYBURGER. Ooh! I'll have you all arrested! You're doing this on purpose. This is my first case and you're all trying to ruin it for me!

TOM. Mr. Fryburger, sit down. I'll tell you everything.

BILLY. Not everything.

TOM. Yes.

BILLY. You mean I spent the whole day running around dressed like this for nothing?

TOM. Yes.

BILLY. I'm going to kill you.

TOM. Fine, but let me explain everything first. He deserves that much. You're going to laugh when you hear this. You see, Mr. Fryburger, my brother and I are dirt poor. We work in an Exxon station pumping gas. I like to play the horses. I like it a little too much. I kind of spent Billy's entire life savings away on bets. And I borrowed from a loan shark to bet some more. He's threatened to kill us if we didn't pay him back by today. When I knew grandfather's will was going to be read, we decided to kidnap Lisa, stick her with novacaine, hole her up in the wall and take her inheritance.

BILLY. We gave her sandwiches and Dr. Pepper.

TOM. But then Lisa showed up and we didn't know she'd have a baby!

BILLY. So I pretended to be dead and we tied her up and stuck her in the closet instead.

TOM. But what we didn't know is that Lisa really is a nun.

BILLY. So she can't have a baby!

TOM. Right. Then the Mother Superior called, which scared the hell out of us.

BILLY. And Pizza Face showed up with a gun.

TOM. So we knocked him out and wanted to rob the safe to pay him back.

BILLY. Before he killed us.

TOM. But before we did, he disappeared and you caught us. And...that's all there is to it.

FRYBURGER. Oh, that's all there is to it?

TOM & BILLY. Yes.

FRYBURGER. You're all going to jail! Fraud is a very serious offense.

JANE. No. I don't think any charges will be pressed.

FRYBURGER. Oh, you don't. And why is that?

JANE. Because I really am Lisa Buckle.

TOM. You are Lisa Buckle.

BILLY. You said Lisa was a nun.

JANE. Yeah, well... I lied. Mr. Fryburger, if you'd done your job correctly, you'd have screened our backgrounds very carefully. The inheritance is mine and I'll do as I like with it. They didn't fraud me as far as I'm concerned.

FRYBURGER. I don't need your permission to have them arrested. With or without your permission, they committed a fraud.

TOM. You really are Lisa?

JANE. I'm afraid so.

TOM. Then why didn't you help us from the beginning? Why did you let us sweat this thing out all day?

JANE. What did you expect me to do? I walk in here and overhear that someone claiming to be me is tied up in the closet. I wanted to find out why. And the more

I found out, the more fun it became. I told you, I love adventure. I had a ball.

(**JANE** *laughs.*)

BILLY. Then, you aren't really a nurse.

JANE. Of course not.

BILLY. Then, I don't really have mumps.

JANE. Of course not.

BILLY. *(Brightening.)* Oh, I feel so much better now.

JANE. Can I ask something? *(To* **GIRL.***)* Who are you?

GIRL. I sell Avon. Then this isn't really a sanitarium?

BILLY. Of course not. Tom just told you that so you wouldn't give us away. You're an Avon Lady?

GIRL. I have to support little Russell somehow. After my husband…

FRYBURGER. Died!!!!

GIRL. Yes! I became an Avon Lady. I figured with all the money flowing around here today, I could make a few bucks.

TOM. I'm sorry you had to go through all of this today.

GIRL. Oh, that's okay. I got to meet Billy out of it.

BILLY. Can I change now? I'm sweating buckets in this thing.

TOM. Don't sweat in it, too much. We have to return it to Sister Rose Marie at St. Agnes.

BILLY. What did you tell her to get her to lend it to you?

TOM. I didn't actually tell her anything. She had her car door open and a lot of laundry inside. I kind of borrowed it.

BILLY. You stole from a nun! You are low. You are beneath low! You are underground you are so low!

TOM. Underground?

FRYBURGER. I must tell you what I think of you. You are utterly contemptible. I find your ethics disgusting. I can't wait to have you arrested. You deserve to be in jail!

TOM. You think I'm proud? I know I'm disgusting.

BILLY. All you think about is saving yourself. All you think about is yourself.

TOM. Well, somebody's got to think of me.

BILLY. Maybe if you started thinking of other people for a change, somebody'd start thinking about you.

TOM. There happens to be somebody thinking of me right this minute.

JANE. I'm ashamed to admit it, but it's true...

TOM. ...Pizza Face Petrillo. I only did this today out of desperation. You have to understand that. What's everybody blaming me for, anyway? Billy was in this as much as I was.

BILLY. You hit me in the head so much, everything's loose in there. *(To the others.)* Did I know what I was doing?

TOM. I'll hit you in the head...

JANE. Tom, let's go find this guy and pay him off. I don't want to see you both killed.

BILLY. I'm gonna go put some pants on.

(**BILLY** *starts up the stairs.*)

TOM. You could have said no, Billy. Just remember that. You could have said no.

BILLY. Yeah? How many nuns do you know who wear pants, smarty?

(**BILLY** *exits as* **TOM** *tries to figure out what he said.*)

JANE. Come on, let's open the safe and get out of here.

FRYBURGER. Just a minute. You aren't going anywhere. We have something to settle here.

JANE. You can postpone arresting them for a few hours.

FRYBURGER. I'm afraid not. I got burned rather badly myself tonight. No hard feelings.

GIRL. Surely you can wait a few hours.

TOM. God knows you've had practice.

FRYBURGER. Tell you what I'll do. I'll give you the freedom to leave, providing I get something in return. In advance.

TOM. Anything. Anything.

FRYBURGER. I was supposed to rendezvous with a certain young lady upstairs in her bedroom tonight. I'd like to complete that rendezvous.

JANE. What?

FRYBURGER. Take it or leave it. It's a matter of life and death now, isn't it?

TOM. You're saying that if Jane goes upstairs with you, you'll drop all charges and let us out of here?

FRYBURGER. Precisely.

TOM. Do it. Do it.

GIRL. Tom!

JANE. I will not!

TOM. Oh, go ahead. What am I saying?

(TOM bravely puts his arm around JANE.)

Go ahead, Mr. Fryburger. Turn us in!

(As FRYBURGER reaches for the phone, PIZZA FACE bursts in from the wine cellar. He still wears his underclothes, his guns drawn.)

PIZZA FACE. Everybody against the wall. It's all over now.

(Everyone heads for the wall, in fear for their lives.)

I don't know what kind of place this is, but I ain't sticking around here no more. You got the money, Buckle?

TOM. Well...

(TOM vainly feels in his pockets for the cash.)

PIZZA FACE. All right. Give me your pants.

(In fear for his own life, FRYBURGER drops his pajama pants to his feet.)

TOM. What?

PIZZA FACE. Your pants. I ain't leaving here looking like this.

(TOM takes his pants off and hands them to PIZZA FACE, who puts them on.)

TOM. They're very expensive pants...

(JANE, the GIRL, and FRYBURGER turn around to see his expensive pants.)

Surely they must be worth...

PIZZA FACE. Hey, I told you people. Against the wall!

GIRL. Is that?

JANE. It is!

GIRL. Any particular wall?

PIZZA FACE. Move it. *(To FRYBURGER.)* Nice pajamas.

TOM. That's it. We're all goners now.

PIZZA FACE. I'll ask again. Do you have my money on you? Yes or no?

TOM. Me?

(TOM feels for the cash in pockets that he no longer has.)

You're not going to believe this, but...no. *(To JANE.)* You happy? I finally told the truth.

JANE. Now? You pick now to tell the truth? One more lie wouldn't have hurt.

(TOM points to JANE.)

TOM. She has the money. *(To JANE.)* How was that?

(PIZZA FACE advances to JANE gun drawn.)

JANE. Not on me, I don't.

(JANE points to FRYBURGER.)

He has the money.

FRYBURGER. (Face *into wall, in fear.*) Actually, I don't. Nothing gets transferred until tomorrow and I don't have the authority or the combination of the...

>   (**PIZZA FACE** *advances to the* **GIRL**.)

PIZZA FACE. How much you got on you?

GIRL. About seventeen dollars. And a box of lipsticks.

TOM. *(Desperate.)* How about the kid?

JANE. I've got $130.

FRYBURGER. *(Into wall.)* All I've got are my plastic cards.

TOM. Let's see, that makes about $147. I don't suppose you'll accept this with a sincere apology?

PIZZA FACE. You supposed right, dead man.

>   *(From above,* **BILLY** *re-enters, in habit... Still wearing his eyebrows and mustache.)*

JANE. Aah.

TOM. Be brave, Jane.

BILLY. I can't find my pants!

>   *(***PIZZA FACE** *and* **BILLY** *meet eyes.* **TOM**, **FRYBURGER**, **JANE**, *and the* **GIRL** *assume firing squad positions.* **BILLY** *thinks he is about to meet his doom.* **PIZZA FACE**, *however, hides his gun and addresses him.)*

PIZZA FACE. Oh, good evening, Sister Fernando.

BILLY. Hellooooo, my son.

PIZZA FACE. What's all over your face?

BILLY. My skin. What's all over your face?

PIZZA FACE. There's grease or something on your face.

FRYBURGER. Sister Fernando is an ace mechanic.

BILLY. Yes. And I was just rotating my tires.

PIZZA FACE. A nun and a mechanic? Hey, can you turn oil into wine?

>   *(Laughs.)*

BILLY. No, but I can make a fool out of a moron.

>   *(He laughs,* **PIZZA FACE** *joins in.)*

PIZZA FACE. Ha ha. Wait. What?

BILLY. What seems to be going on here?

Well, sir, the late Theodore Buckle has left this estate to us and we're turning it into the "Theodore Buckle Orphanage of Brotherly Love."

PIZZA FACE. An orphanage?

BILLY. *(Scared.)* Yes. Would you buy that?

> *(**TOM**, **FRYBURGER**, **JANE**, and the **GIRL** assume firing squad positions.)*

PIZZA FACE. I can't afford to buy it, but I'd be glad to donate. You see, Sister, I was an orphan once myself. When I was a kid. Me and my brother Leonard. The other kids always made fun of Leonard. They called him S.S. Leonard 'cause he always wet the bed. Every night he'd wet that bed. And we shared that bed. I had to sleep in that bed. I'd wake up screaming, "I'm drowning! I'm drowning!" It was a traumatic thing for a kid to wake up in the night after Leonard had done it again. The good Sisters who ran that orphanage helped us through the rough times. They gave me my own bed. And they gave Leonard an inner tube to sleep with. I'll never forget them for it. *(Teary.)* I miss those good Sisters. I think orphanages are great for orphans.

BILLY. Well, it's hard to argue that.

> *(**PIZZA FACE** reaches into his sock and pulls out a stack of bills.)*

PIZZA FACE. Here, Sister. Five G's for Leonard and me.

BILLY. Oh I couldn't accept that.

TOM. Oh yes you could.

BILLY. *(Taking the bills.)* And where is Leonard today?

PIZZA FACE. Why he's Chief of Police in Bayonne, New Jersey.

> *(**FRYBURGER**, crying, holds out a five dollar bill.)*

FRYBURGER. Sister, I'd like to donate five dollars myself.

PIZZA FACE. Were you an orphan too?

FRYBURGER. No, actually, it's a tax write-off.

PIZZA FACE. And now, if you'll excuse us, we've got some unfinished business here.

TOM. Oh, don't go, Sister. Stay and recite those ten commandments. Especially my favorite "Thou Shalt Not Kill."

BILLY. Bless you, Mr. Petrillo.

PIZZA FACE. *(In tears.)* It's a pleasure to do something for the little children, Sister. I can't tell you how much those nuns meant to Leonard and me. It's my way of saying thank you.

> *(**PIZZA FACE** falls to his knees, in tears. As he sobs, **BILLY** hands the roll of bills to the **GIRL**, who hands it to **JANE** who hands it to **FRYBURGER**, who tries putting the money in his pocket. **JANE** slaps him and he passes the money along to **TOM**.)*

BILLY. We can never thank you enough. You can rise now.

PIZZA FACE. *(Rising.)* Forgive me, Sister. But I'm such a sentimental guy.

TOM. Well, there's no sense detaining you any longer, Mr. Petrillo. I believe this should take care of our business transaction.

PIZZA FACE. *(Accepting the money back.)* I thought you didn't have it on you.

TOM. It was just hard to get at.

> *(**PIZZA FACE** counts up his money.)*

PIZZA FACE. Thank you, Mr. Buckle. You're a gentleman. It's been a pleasure dealing with you. I hope we do business again. Soon.

TOM. Sorry. But I have learned my lesson.

BILLY. You have?

TOM. Jane... Lisa? If you'll forgive me, I promise I'll never gamble again.

JANE. I find that hard to believe.

TOM. I'll bet you I don't.

JANE. I forgive you.

FRYBURGER. Well, don't let us keep you here, Mr. Petrillo.

PIZZA FACE. Hey, do I know you?

FRYBURGER. I hardly think so.

PIZZA FACE. I do know you! You're Knuckles Fryburger, aren't you? Aren't you Knuckles Fryburger?

BILLY. Knuckles?

FRYBURGER. The name is Robert Fryburger. You must have me mistaken for someone else.

PIZZA FACE. You used to run numbers for Lucky Gonza.

(All eyes turn to look at **"KNUCKLES" FRYBURGER.***)*

FRYBURGER. *(Trapped.)* It's a lie! It's... I... I...

JANE. You just lost your rendezvous, tiger.

BILLY. Mr. Fryburger! You, a numbers runner.

FRYBURGER. Do you have any idea how expensive law school is? How else could I afford it?

TOM. Looks like we're even, Knuckles. You don't tell on us and we won't tell on you.

*(***PIZZA FACE*** knocks on cellar door.)*

PIZZA FACE. Virginia! Let's get going! *(To the others.)* Whoever thought I'd find a doll like her in a joint like this?

*(***VIRGINIA*** enters from the cellar, all dolled up in a neon-lime evening dress. Her make-up is extra thick. She wears a flower in her hair and carries a carpet bag.)*

VIRGINIA. Here I am, lover boy.

BILLY. Virginia, you're leaving with him?

VIRGINIA. Sorry I won't be able to stay on here. I've got something much more important now. And he's Italian. I'm his new secretary. Sister, you were right.

*(***MISS MACKINTOSH*** enters, fuming mad.)*

MACKINTOSH. Hey! What's going on here?

PIZZA FACE. MacKintosh! Gimme those car keys.

(**PIZZA FACE** *grabs them from her cleavage.*)

MACKINTOSH. You two-timing creep.

PIZZA FACE. *(To* **VIRGINIA**.*)* You wanna swig before we go?

VIRGINIA. I've got my own, lover boy.

(**VIRGINIA** *pulls bottles from her carpet bag.*)

Goodbye, Mr. Buckle!

(**VIRGINIA** *and* **PIZZA FACE** *exit together.*)

MACKINTOSH. *(Calling after.)* Hey! What about me? I've been sitting in that car all night. That two-timing creep. Now what do I have? Nothing! No singing contract. I don't even have a ride home. How do you like them apples!

FRYBURGER. *(Eying her.)* Oh, I do. I do. I'd be more than happy to drive you wherever you like. I was just leaving myself.

MACKINTOSH. You need a sec-a-tary?

FRYBURGER. I'm sure we can work something out. You know, I could use a legal secretary.

MACKINTOSH. That's me. I'm a secatary.

FRYBURGER. Sec-re-tary.

MACKINTOSH. Sec-a-tary. I've never been a legal secatary before. I ain't never been a legal nothing before.

TOM. Don't forget your pants Knuckles.

FRYBURGER. Someone from my office will be over tomorrow to transfer the estate Miss Buckle. I want to tell you all, quite honestly, that I'm very truly sorry.

TOM. Oh, that's okay.

FRYBURGER. I'm sorry you're all not in jail!! Let's go. Miss MacKintosh. My clothes are upstairs.

MACKINTOSH. Oh, you won't need them. You're cuter than that little homely one.

BILLY. He's not homely!

(**FRYBURGER** *and* **MACKINTOSH** *exit up the stairs.*)

GIRL. That's right.

TOM. I told you I could handle any situation.

BILLY. You didn't handle anything. This was the most ill-conceived, badly executed, most ridiculously stupid thing anyone's ever tried to pull off.

TOM. So maybe I like to do things the hard way. At least I got to meet Jane… Lisa out of it. Do you believe in love at first sight?

JANE. Not at all.

TOM. Oh.

BILLY. I know I do. I'm in love with an Avon Lady!

GIRL. I can't wait to show you my samples.

BILLY. Ooh.

JANE. At least we know who everybody is now.

BILLY. Yeah. I'm Billy. And that's Tom. And you're Lisa. And that's Little Russell. And you're…

GIRL. Pam.

BILLY. Pam? That's my all-time favorite name!

>   (**BILLY** *and the* **GIRL** *kiss.*)

JANE. Tell me honestly, Tom. Would you be in love with me if I was poor?

TOM. Honestly? You know I would.

JANE. You would?

TOM. Sure. But I'd keep my mouth shut about it.

>   (*Telephone rings.*)

>   (**BILLY** *and the* **GIRL** *part their kiss. She now wears the black tape mustache.* **TOM** *answers the phone.*)

Hello? Buckle residence… Just a minute.
Billy, it's for you.

>   (**BILLY** *heads for the phone.*)

BILLY. Who is it?

>   (**TOM** *begins to hand the receiver to him.*)

TOM. It's your Mother Superior.

> (**TOM** *realizes what he's just said.* **BILLY** *and* **TOM** *do takes to the phone and each other.* **JANE** *smiles.*)

(Curtain.)

End of Play

PROPERTY LIST

PRE-SET:
    AT BAR; Fully stocked bar, decanters, ice, glasses.
    ON TEA CART; Tray with big dome-lid covering hors d'oeuvres.
    ON TABLE STAGE LEFT; Telephone.
    IN BOOKCASE; Two removable books, pint bottle of booze, ¼ full.
    IN HALLWAY (UPSTAGE RIGHT); Two suitcases – one filled with two pieces of rope and a gag, and a large needle. A briefcase filled with will, pads, papers and pens. A nickel attached to the will. Wrapped baby and sample bag.
    OFFSTAGE RIGHT (WINE CELLAR); Two empty booze bottles, carpet bag filled with liquor bottles.
    OFFSTAGE LEFT (CONSERVATORY); Gun, roll of bills, car keys, chewing gum.
    IN BEDROOMS (UPSTAGE LEFT); Two flashlights, map of estate, nun habit and wimple.
    COVERING SOFA, CHAIR, BAR, TEA TRAY AND VASE STAND; Drop cloths.
    BY STAIRCASE; Vase stand with breakaway vase.

AFTER ACT I – Scene One:
    Remove dropcloths.

END ACT I:
    Set breakaway bottle at bar.

END ACT II:
    Clean away breakaway vase and bottle. Set baby offstage left, set car keys off upstage right.

PERSONAL PROPS:
    TOM; watch.
    FRYBURGER; watch, $5 bill.
    GIRL; watch.
    PIZZA FACE; gun, roll of money, keys.
    MACKINTOSH; chewing gum.

SOUND EFFECTS

Telephone ring.
Doorbell.
Baby cry.

COSTUME PLOT
BILLY

ACT I – Scene One
Black turtleneck, Black pants, white socks, white tennis sneakers.

ACT I – Scene Two
White shirt, tie, black pants, white socks, brown check jacket, sneakers.
into
Black robe, white bib, black & white wimple, same socks and sneakers.
into
Street clothes.
into
Nun habit, adding baby under robe at chest height.

ACT II
Nun habit.
into
Street clothes.
into
Nun habit.
into
Street clothes.

ACT III
Same as Act One – Scene One.
into
Nun habit.

TOM

ACT I – Scene One
Black turtleneck, black pants, black socks and shoes.

ACT I – Scene Two
White shirt, tie, black pants, black socks and shoes, green check jacket.

ACT II
Same.

ACT III
Black turtleneck, black pants, black socks and shoes, red check boxer shorts.

JANE

ACTS I AND II
White and blue flowered sweater, blue skirt, white heels, pearls.

ACT III
Black t-shirt, black slacks, black heels, pearls.

FRYBURGER
ACTS I AND II
Blue shirt, navy jacket, grey vest, grey pants, black socks and shoes, watch.

ACT III
Red and white striped pajamas, red slippers, watch, blue check boxer shorts.

VIRGINIA
ACTS I AND II
Grey maid uniform, white apron, black fishnet stockings, red shoes, cheap curly black wig (worn with grey strands of real hair coming through at hairline).
Heavy make-up (Bette Davis in *Whatever Happened to Baby Jane*) and big false eyelashes.

ACT III
Bright pink maribu negligee, with pink slippers.
into
Loud line-green evening gown, with matching maribu jacket, red shoes, red flower in hair, dangle earrings.

GIRL
ENTIRE SHOW
Pastel skirt and blouse, heels. Should wear bright nail polish, watch and bracelets. Hair should be worn up to ease tying a gag.

PIZZA FACE
ACT II
Blue pin-striped suit, wide-brimmed hat, red shirt, red and blue tie, red silk handkerchief, black socks with garters, two-tone shoes, pinky ring.

ACT III
Blue silk guinea-t-shirt, bright blue boxers, black socks with garters, wide-brimmed hat, pinky ring, two-tone shoes.

MISS MACKINTOSH
ENTIRE SHOW
Tight red wrap-around dress (low cut), red heels. Should wear cheap peroxide blonde wig, big lashes, gawdy jewelry and dangle earrings.

www.ingramcontent.com/pod-product-compliance
Lightning Source LLC
Chambersburg PA
CBHW051405290426
44108CB00015B/2160